TEENS IMAGE

From Inputs to Identity

AF510690

BlueRose ONE.com
Stories Matter
NewDelhi • London

BLUEROSE PUBLISHERS
India | U.K.

For permissions requests or inquiries regarding this publication, please contact:

BLUEROSE PUBLISHERS
www.BlueRoseONE.com
info@bluerosepublishers.com
+91 8882 898 898
+4407342408967

ISBN: 978-93-7139-088-0

First Edition: July 2025

📕 Preface

This book isn't just a collection of words—it's a mirror, a guide, and a friend.
It was written with one simple but powerful goal:
To help you understand how your senses, thoughts, and small daily actions shape the bigger picture of your life.

In a world full of noise, pressure, and confusion, this book offers clarity.
It combines timeless wisdom with modern-day experiences—crafted especially for teens who are still discovering who they are and what they can become.

You won't find lectures here.
You'll find conversations, questions, and reflections that speak directly to your heart and your reality.

Because when you understand the signals your body and mind are giving you every day, you begin to take control—
Not just of your habits, but of your entire life direction.

But today's world?
It's louder. Faster. More distracting.
Teens like you face constant noise—outside and inside.
So I felt it was time to give that ancient wisdom a modern, clear, and practical voice.

You're now holding the **27th version** of this book.
Yes—I failed 26 times before this one.
Not because I didn't know what I wanted to say,
But because the feelings in my heart and the thoughts in my mind were too deep to express easily.

Each version was a battle—between emotion and expression, between soul and structure.
But this version? This one… it clicked.
I laughed. I cried.
I felt like a teacher finally speaking clearly from the heart.

These words are mine—my emotions, my logic, my journey.
But I wrote them for you.

Over the last **4 years**, I've spoken to thousands of students—
Listened to their struggles, confusions, fears, and silent pain points.
And I realized one thing clearly: **our education doesn't always teach us how to understand ourselves**.
So I took it upon myself to create something that could help.

I'm a **self-learner**. I don't hold formal degrees in psychology or spiritual science.
But I hold something just as powerful: **curiosity, dedication, and lived experience**.
This book was not born in a classroom. It was born in moments of silence, struggle, observation—and in conversations with real teens like you.

So if one day someone questions:
"How did you write about this without a certificate?"
Here's my honest answer:
I didn't wait for permission to understand life. I studied it myself—and now I'm sharing it with you.

So, **baccha**, let's begin.
Let's dive into the journey of *TEENS IMAGE*.

📖 Introduction

1. The Power of TEENS – Why the 5 Senses Are Your Superpowers

Wait… I know what you're thinking.
"TEENS" means teenagers—right?
Thirteen to nineteen. School life, selfies, crushes, rebellion, and figuring yourself out.

That's what most people assume.

But here's the twist:
In this book, **TEENS** stands for something much deeper:

T.E.E.N.S. – Tongue, Eyes, Ears, Nose, Skin
These are your **five senses**.

Your five superpowers.

Every second, they are shaping your **IMAGE**—inside and out.
What you taste, see, hear, smell, and touch is constantly building your world—both your **outer reality** and your **inner identity**.

Yes, I named it *TEENS* so it would feel relatable to teenagers like you.
But this book isn't just for scrolling or finishing in one sitting.
It's not a "quick read"—it's a **journey**.

A journey of understanding who you really are—
Not by copying trends, but by discovering how your senses are programming your personality.

So take your time, **baccha**.
Underline. Highlight. Pause. Reflect. Re-read.
Enjoy the ride.

Because once you understand your **T.E.E.N.S.**,
You'll finally know how to shape your true **I.M.A.G.E.**.

---

2. Why Teens? – The Most Sensitive and Formative Phase

Between ages 13 and 19, your brain is like **wet cement**—soft, moldable, and incredibly quick at learning.

What you allow into your system during these years has a **deep and lasting impact**.

This is the phase when you begin to ask yourself:

- Who am I, really?
- How do others see me?
- Why do I feel this way?
- What do I want to become?

Whether you realize it or not, your answers are being shaped by the **sensory input** around you—what you eat, watch, hear, smell, and feel every day.

So if you want different answers, you have to start by becoming **aware of your inputs**.

---

3. The Double Meaning of IMAGE

This book talks a lot about **IMAGE**.
But not just in one way—it has **two layers** of meaning:

• **Outer IMAGE**

How you appear to the world. Your behavior, style, and presence.

• **Inner IMAGE**

Your thoughts, beliefs, emotions, habits, and self-confidence.

But there's one more surprising meaning.

Scientifically, **IMAGE** stands for:
Integrated Molecular Analysis of Gene Expression

In simple terms?
It means your environment—through your senses—can influence how your **genes express themselves**.

Your surroundings are not just decorating your life—they're **programming it**.
Your sensory world is silently building the person you're becoming.

---

4. How This Book Works – Interactive, Practical, and Personal

This book isn't just for reading.
It's for **experiencing**.

Each chapter includes:

- Clear logic and science behind each sense
- Real world stories and examples
- Visual diagrams and tools for deeper understanding
- 4–5 short, powerful quotes to reflect and share
- A chapter progress bar to see how far you've come

You'll also find:

- **Journaling prompts** to explore your personal IMAGE
- **Sense-check audits** to become aware of what you're absorbing

- **Visualization and reprogramming exercises** to upgrade your mental patterns

This book isn't a lecture—it's a **conversation between us**.

By the time you finish, you won't just *understand* the TEENS IMAGE—you'll feel like you've **built it with your own hands**.

CONTENTS

📕 PART 1: TEENS – The 5 Sensory Inputs

Chapter 1: T - Tongue (Taste & Speech)........14

- Taste: Food and habits
- Speech: Self-talk, affirmations, and spoken influence

Chapter 2: E - Eyes (Sight)........27

- Social media, role models, fashion, body image
- Visual environment and exposure

Chapter 3: E - Ears (Hearing)........34

- Music, advice, gossip, encouragement
- Mental noise vs. mindful listening

Chapter 4: N - Nose (Smell)........40

- Scents and memories
- Emotional comfort, identity through scent

Chapter 5: S - Skin (Touch)......47

- Physical contact, safety, comfort
- Emotional sensitivity through skin

Part 1: Summary

🛠 PART 2: Building Your IMAGE

Chapter 6: Inner IMAGE vs Outer IMAGE......56

- Self-perception vs. how others see you
- Emotional blueprint & physical identity

Chapter 7: Habits Like Code......63

- Gene expression metaphor
- Repeating actions = programming identity

Chapter 8: The Science Behind IMAGE......69

- Brain development in teens
- Neuroplasticity, sensory memory, emotional learning

Part 2: Summary

✨ PART 3: Shaping a Positive IMAGE

Chapter 9: Sense-Check Audit Activity......79

- Daily check-ins for each sense
- Reflect: what are you consuming and expressing?

Chapter 10: Reflection Exercises......86

- Journaling your IMAGE
- Identify patterns & emotional triggers

Chapter 11: Visualization & Reprogramming......93

- Mental rehearsal, guided visualizations
- Resetting internal narratives

Chapter 12: Choosing Your Influences......101

- Environment, friends, media
- Conscious input = conscious growth

Chapter 13: Reprogramming Negative Patterns...109

- Overcoming toxic inputs
- Replacing destructive with constructive

Part 3: Summary

🌍 PART 4: Real-World Applications

Chapter 14: TEENS IMAGE at School...121

- Academic identity, peer pressure
- How sensory input shapes learning confidence

Chapter 15: Social Media & Digital Persona...128

- Filters vs. authenticity
- Creating mindful digital presence

Chapter 16: Friendships & Dating...134

- Emotional boundaries, sensory chemistry
- Respect, communication, connection

Chapter 17: Mental Health Awareness..**141**

- How sensory overload affects stress & anxiety
- Mindful breaks, emotional hygiene

Chapter 18: Confidence & Public Image..**148**

- Posture, tone, clothes, energy
- How to carry your IMAGE confidently

Part 4: Summary

🔚 FINAL PART:

Chapter 19: Create Your IMAGE Vision Board..**159**

- Visual map of your desired IMAGE
- Break down into small habits

Chapter 20: Walking Together – Final Words..**165**

- "If you've seen my image, I'm walking with you."
- Your journey ahead, and revisiting this book over time

Finale Part Summary

1.

The Tongue — More Than Just Taste

Taste – Food and Habits

The Power of Your Tongue Begins with Taste

The tongue is your body's taste decoder—able to sense **sweet, salty, sour, bitter,** and **umami (savory)**. But it's not just helping you enjoy food; it's influencing your thoughts, actions, and even your long-term habits.

When you take a bite of something—let's say chocolate or masala chips—your taste buds send a message through the **facial** and **glossopharyngeal nerves** directly to your brain. The brain responds by releasing **dopamine**, the feel-good chemical. This forms a *memory of pleasure*, and your brain remembers:

> "This felt good. Let's do it again."

And just like that, a simple snack becomes a *loop*—a pattern.

♻️ The Taste Habit Loop

Let's break down how taste builds habits:

1. **You eat something that tastes good**
2. **You feel pleasure (dopamine hit)**
3. **You want it again (craving starts)**
4. **You repeat it (habit forms)**

Soon, you're no longer eating to fuel your body—you're eating because your brain *expects pleasure*.

From Hunger to Habit

Food is supposed to energize, nourish, and balance the body. But now? It often serves a different purpose:

- Escaping boredom
- Rewarding stress
- Filling emotional gaps

You eat not because you're hungry, but because it's **available**, **tastes good**, or simply out of **habit**.

This unconscious loop is something 99% of people fall into daily—without even realizing it.

> 🎯 *"You're not what you eat—you're what you repeat."*

🧘 The Shift: From Taste Craving to Conscious Eating

Here's the game-changer:
Before your next bite, ask:

> **"Am I eating because I need it—or just because it's tasty or available?"**

That one question flips the habit.

This is **mindful eating**—where you begin to listen to your **body's demand**, not your tongue's command.

🧪 Food ≠ Always Fuel (An Apple Example)

Let's take a basic example: **An apple.**

🍎 Situation 1: Late Night Snack

You're about to sleep. You see an apple. It feels healthy, right?

But here's the truth:

- Apple contains sugar (fructose), fiber, and vitamin C
- Your body at night is slowing down
- Eating sugar—even natural—can disrupt your sleep cycle

❗ Even healthy food, at the wrong time, becomes **unhelpful**.

🍎 Situation 2: Before Solving a Math Problem

Now, you're prepping for focus and brainwork. The apple here:

- Gives you clean energy
- Boosts hydration
- Feeds your brain glucose
- Doesn't weigh you down

✅ In this case, the same apple is **exactly what your body needs**.

> ⚖️ *"The apple didn't change. Your awareness did."*

🧠 Build Bodywise Eating Habits

It's not just about **what** you eat—but **when and why** you eat.

Ask yourself:

- "Is this food giving me energy or making me lazy?"
- "Am I eating from hunger—or habit?"
- "Is my next action physical, mental, or restful?"

This awareness is your *superpower.*

🧬 Teen Bodies, Teen Brains

As a teen, your body is still *coding itself.* Hormones, brain circuits, bones, and even your skin are still forming. The food you choose now directly affects:

- Mood swings and confidence
- Focus and school performance
- Sleep quality and skin health
- Long-term shape, energy, and strength

💥 *"Your future body is being built one bite at a time."*

⚠️ Before You Eat: Do a Quick Body Check-In

Ask yourself:

- What am I about to do next? (Sleep? Study? Workout?)
- Does this food help that action?
- Am I eating this because it's available—or necessary?

📌 *"Availability should not decide your diet—awareness should."*

💪 Discipline on the Tongue = Power in the Brain

Eating consciously may feel slow at first. You'll have to pause. Think. Decide.

And yes—it feels weird in the beginning.

But give it time.

- What was once effort becomes instinct
- What felt unnatural becomes automatic
- What started as a choice becomes your **new code**

🌱 Small Bite, Big Change

Start small:

- Pause before snacking
- Understand your next action
- Match your food to your body's current need

This simple pause is what separates *unhealthy patterns* from *self-mastery*.

> ✨ *"You're not just changing your food—you're changing your future."*

🔁 Visual Summary: The Eating Awareness Loop

```
Taste → Dopamine → Craving → Habit → Pattern →
Health Outcome
↓
Awareness → Pause → Body Check → Smart Choice →
New Pattern
```

📢 Quotes You Can Share - #teensimage

- "Discipline on the tongue builds power in the brain."
- "Eat based on body demand, not taste command."
- "Taste is temporary. Pattern is permanent."
- "Your tongue programs your future, one bite at a time."

🔊 Your Tongue Can Program Your Brain

Words are not just sounds—they're *instructions to your system.* The **tongue** gives voice to your thoughts. And here's the twist:

> The more you speak a thought, the more your brain believes it.

Every word you say is either:

- **Coding your confidence** or
- **Weakening your inner belief**

Let's break this into two main directions speech works in your life:

---

1 Self-Talk: What You Say to Yourself

This is the most **constant voice** in your life.

It's what you say when no one's watching:

- "I'm not good at this."
- "Why do I always mess up?"
- "I knew I'd fail..."

Or:

- "I'll figure it out."
- "I'm improving every day."
- "This challenge is shaping me."

Which one do you use more?

💡 *Your self-talk is your self-hypnosis.*

🧠 The Science Behind Self-Talk

Your brain listens to your language.
When you say "I can't," it reduces effort.
When you say "I will try," it activates problem-solving.
When you say "I'm improving," it creates momentum.

This is how **neuroplasticity** works:
What you *repeat*, your brain *rewires*.

📣 Affirmations: Speak What You Want to Become

Affirmations are not just "positive quotes"—they're **training commands**.

By saying:

- "I am confident"
- "I stay calm under pressure"

- "I deserve respect"

You start creating a new *mental circuit*—one that influences your posture, choices, reactions, and mindset.

> 🔁 *What you say ➜ shapes what you believe ➜ decides what you become*

---

2 Spoken Influence: What You Say to Others

Your words also shape the world *around* you.

In school, in a group chat, or at home—your words can either:

- Uplift others
- Tear someone down
- Reflect your insecurity
- Express your confidence

People judge not just what you say—but **how you say it**.

🧭 Speech Reveals Your Inner Image

Examples:

- Do you gossip or inspire?
- Do you speak out of ego or awareness?

- Do you listen to respond, or listen to understand?

The way you speak reveals whether your inner image is **insecure or solid**, **agitated or aligned**.

🔑 Mastering the Pause Before Speaking

Here's a simple, life-changing rule:

> ✋ *"Pause before you speak."*

Why?

Because **your first thought is emotional**, but your **second thought is usually wiser**.

That one-second pause can:

- Save a friendship
- Avoid a fight
- Build your respect
- Show maturity beyond your age

> 🎯 *Power is not just in speaking fast—it's in speaking with awareness.*

🛡️ Words Can Heal or Hurt (Choose Wisely)

- A cruel joke can cause a person years of self-doubt.
- A sincere compliment can uplift someone for life.
- Your words are like *swords or seeds*—what are you throwing?

🧘 How to Practice Better Speech Daily

Try this:

1. **Silent Check-In:** Before speaking, pause and check—*Is it kind? Is it useful? Is it necessary?*
2. **Voice Journaling:** Speak affirmations into your phone daily like:
   "I am enough." "I learn quickly." "I bring peace when I speak."
3. **Use Powerful Phrases:**
   - Instead of "I can't," say "I'm still learning."
   - Instead of "This is hard," say "This will grow me."
   - Instead of "I'm bad at this," say "I'm getting better each time."

💥 Words Shape Reality

Think of your **tongue as a creator**.

- It can break your own confidence—or build it
- It can damage someone's day—or make their week
- It can start a fight—or open a friendship
- It can echo pain—or broadcast peace

🔗 *Words don't just describe your reality. They create it.*

📢 Quotes You Can Share - #teensimage

- *"Your words are instructions to your future."*
- *"Self-talk is self-programming—watch your language."*
- *"Speak not to impress, but to express the truth with care."*
- *"The tongue has no bones—but it can break or build lives."*

📶 Progress Gauge.

2.

The Eyes — Your Inner Camera

🎬 Introduction: Your Eyes Are More Than Just Lenses

Your **eyes** don't just help you *see the world.*
They also help you **build your world**.

Every second, your eyes are capturing **information**, **colors**, **shapes**, **faces**, and **screens**—and sending them straight to your brain.

But here's the truth:

> **You don't just see with your eyes.**
> **You build beliefs with your eyes.**

🧠 How the Eye Connects to the Brain

When you look at something—whether it's a person, a phone screen, or a mirror—your **retina** captures that image and sends it to your **visual cortex**.

Your brain:

- Interprets it
- Stores it
- Reacts to it

So in a way, you're not just seeing the world...
You're **recording** it.
You're **memorizing** how to feel, think, or act based on what your eyes repeatedly take in.

📺 What You See, You Start to Become

Ever noticed how:

- After watching a fitness reel, you feel like working out?
- After watching gossip content, your mind gets negative?
- After watching someone confident, you adjust your posture?

That's **mirror neuron activity** at work—your brain **copies** what it sees.

Repetition becomes reflection.
What you watch again and again becomes your **inner image**.

The Eyes and Body Image

This is a big one—especially for teens.

When you constantly see:

- Edited bodies
- Perfect skin
- Six-packs or zero-figure models

You start **comparing** yourself.
You start **judging** your worth.

But remember:

> *Social media is not real life. It's a highlight reel.*
> Most of it is **filtered**, **posed**, or **designed to trigger envy.**

So stop using fake standards to judge your real self.

The Eyes Can Fool You — If You Let Them

Your eyes are **powerful**, but not always **wise**.

They show you:

- What's outside—not what's true inside.

- What's flashy—not what's valuable.
- What others have—not what you can become.

🧠 *Discernment* comes when you train your **mind to lead**, not your **eyes to decide**.

💡 The Secret Trick: Control What You Feed Your Eyes

You don't always control what you *see in the world*.

But you **do** control what you *choose to watch, scroll, read, or focus on*.

Just like food shapes the body, **visual input shapes the mind**.

So ask:

- Are you watching things that uplift you or drain you?
- Are you seeing things that teach you or distract you?
- Are you using your eyes to grow—or just to scroll?

🔄 Let's Look at Two Situations

📱 Situation 1: Scrolling Reels Before Study Time

You think: "Just 5 minutes."

You end up watching:

- 20 funny clips
- 5 gym videos
- 3 outfit changes
- 2 people fighting

Your brain is now:

- **Overstimulated**
- **Distracted**
- **Craving dopamine**

Now try to study… it's 10x harder.
Not because you're lazy—but because your brain is **visually drunk**.

📓 Situation 2: Watching a TED Talk or Calm Nature Clip

You take 5 minutes to:

- Watch something inspiring
- Listen to someone's real journey
- Or even stare at a calm mountain lake

Now you feel:

- Grounded
- Inspired
- Ready to focus

Same 5 minutes, different input.

The **difference isn't time—it's choice**.

🧭 Train Your Eyes to Build Your Future

Want to change your mindset?
Start with your **eyesight habits**.

- Follow people who make you think, not just look.
- Observe nature—not just notifications.
- Spend time **looking within**, not just outside.

> 🔍 *True vision is not just looking—it's seeing with understanding.*

📢 Quotes You Can Share - #teensimage

- "What you see daily becomes your definition of normal."
- "Train your eyes, and your thoughts will follow."
- "Don't let the feed decide your future."
- "You're not just seeing the world. You're shaping your mind."
- "Be careful what your eyes worship—it will shape your worth."

📶 Progress Gauge.

3.

The Ears — You Become What You Hear

🎧 Introduction: Your Ears Are Always On

unlike your eyes, which close when you sleep…
Your **ears are always listening.** Even while you're dreaming.

And every sound, every word, every voice you hear—
goes straight into your **mind** and starts shaping your **inner software.**

> "The voice you listen to the most becomes your inner voice."

Let that sink in.
Because your ears don't just hear *noise*—they collect **influence**.

🧠 The Science: How Sound Affects the Brain

Your ears pick up **vibrations**—from music, speech, noise, anything.

These vibrations travel through:

- The **eardrum**
- Into the **cochlea**
- Then to your **auditory nerve**, and straight into the **brain**

Here's what happens next:

- If it's loud or exciting → dopamine spikes
- If it's harsh or angry → stress chemicals (like cortisol) rise
- If it's calming or wise → your mind slows down and absorbs it deeper

This means:
Every sound enters your nervous system and either *sharpens you* or *shakes you.*

🗣️ Words Shape Your Inner World

The **words** you hear daily—especially from those close to you—start becoming the script inside your head.

If someone says:

- "You're dumb." → Your brain records it.
- "You'll never make it." → You start to doubt.
- "You got this!" → Your self-belief rises.

"Every voice you allow in is a vote for who you become."

📱 Social Media & Music — What Are You Tuning Into?

Let's be real.

Your playlist, your favorite creators, even your memes— they're **constantly talking to your brain.**

- Music with **dark or violent lyrics**?
  → Triggers aggression or sadness without you realizing it.
- Reels full of **negativity or gossip**?
  → Makes your thoughts judgmental.
- Podcasts, interviews, or affirmations?
  → Makes your mind sharp, positive, and open.

"Your vibe is controlled by your audio input."

🎙️ Real-Life Scenarios

🎧 Situation 1: You Wake Up and Put on a Motivational Podcast

You hear:

- "You are capable."
- "Your past doesn't define your future."

- "Let's win the day."

You now:

- Walk taller
- Think clearer
- Act with intention

This is not magic.
It's just your **ears changing your energy**.

🔊 Situation 2: You Hear Sarcasm, Fights, or Insults All Day

You hear:

- "You're always messing up."
- "What's the point of trying?"
- "This world is garbage."

You now:

- Feel drained
- Start doubting yourself
- Copy that tone in your own thoughts

You're not weak—your environment is loud with negativity.

🧘 The Ears and Peace

Want more peace in life?

You don't need a vacation.
You need to **filter what your ears are exposed to.**

Try this:

- Spend 5 minutes in **silence** each day.
- Turn off **background noise** when studying.
- Use earphones for **positive content only.**

The quieter your outside, the clearer your inside becomes.

💬 Your Inner Voice is a Remix of Outer Voices

Here's the truth:

> The way you talk to yourself… is a remix of everything you've heard so far.

That's why:

- Kids with encouraging parents often believe in themselves.
- Teens who hear only criticism start doubting their worth.
- Those who choose powerful inputs **reprogram their internal voice**.

You get to choose what plays on your inner radio.

Reflection Exercise: Ear Audit

For one day, notice:

- What sounds, words, or music did you hear?
- How did each one make you feel—confident, lazy, stressed, or energized?
- What's one thing you want to cut out—and one thing you want to add?

Quotes You Can Share - #teensimage

- "Your ears are portals. What enters, echoes forever."
- "Don't just listen for fun. Listen to grow."
- "The loudest voice isn't always the wisest."
- "Silence is not empty—it's full of answers."
- "The words you hear the most become the beliefs you live by."

Progress Gauge.

4.

The Nose — Memory's Shortcut to Emotion

🌀 Introduction: Smell is Invisible, But Powerful

Smell is a silent sense.
It doesn't scream like sight. It doesn't buzz like hearing.
But it's always there—**in the background, shaping your feelings**.

You may not notice it…
but your **nose remembers everything your eyes forget.**

Smell is directly wired to the **limbic system**—the brain's emotional center.
This is why just one smell can:

- Take you back to childhood
- Trigger deep joy or sudden sadness
- Make you feel safe, anxious, or even hungry

"Smells don't just enter your nose. They unlock doors inside your mind."

🔬 The Science: Smell, Brain, and Emotion

Your nose detects **chemical particles** in the air and sends signals to the **olfactory bulb**.
But here's the twist:

Unlike other senses, smell **skips the logical brain** and goes straight to the **emotional brain**.

That's why:

- You smell perfume and remember a person.
- You smell rain and feel nostalgic.
- You smell hospital disinfectant and feel uneasy.

Smell = Emotion Trigger
Before you even understand *why*, your mood shifts.

🧠 Smell and Memory

Your brain connects **scents with moments**.

- The smell of your school canteen → memories of lunch with friends

- The smell of incense → childhood prayer time or family rituals
- A specific shampoo → that one relative or friend you miss

These scent-memories are **instant and emotional**.
They're stored deeper than pictures or words.

> "What you smell becomes what you feel—without permission."

🔄 Smell Affects Mood (Without You Realizing)

Let's say:

- You enter a room that **smells clean and fresh** → You feel clear-headed
- You walk into a space that **smells stale or sweaty** → You feel low-energy
- You smell **something burnt or sour** → You feel alert or uncomfortable

Your nose becomes your **body's radar**, alerting you even before you think.
This is why aromatherapy works—smells can calm or energize you naturally.

👃 Two Situations: How Nose Impacts You

Situation 1: You're Anxious Before an Exam

You walk into your room.
There's a calming scent—maybe lavender or sandalwood.

You don't notice it at first.
But within minutes, your breathing slows...
your mind clears up a bit.

Why?

> Your brain associates that scent with calm, comfort, or past focus moments.
> The smell doesn't change your thoughts. It **changes your state**.

Situation 2: You're Studying at a Café

The vibe is great. But the smell of too much food, oil, and sweat starts building.

Suddenly:

- You feel distracted.
- You can't focus.
- You start yawning or feeling uncomfortable.

The reason?

> The **nose is overstimulated**—sending signals to your brain that say, "Escape!"

You thought it was about the seat or the noise...
But it was the smell **changing your mental environment**.

🏠 Smell and Home: Your Emotional Bubble

Every place you live in has a **"smell signature."**
Even your clothes, pillows, books—they hold **emotional scent data**.

When you return home from a trip and smell your pillow, you immediately feel **safe** and **rested**.

This means:
You can *create your emotional climate* by choosing your smell space wisely.

Try these:

- Keep **a clean-smelling corner** for reading or reflecting.
- Use **natural scents** like citrus or sandalwood during journaling.
- Before sleep, try **a calming aroma** to help your nervous system relax.

🧘 Smell & Spiritual Connection

Many ancient traditions used smell to create **sacred focus**:

- **Incense** in temples
- **Camphor** in meditation
- **Essential oils** in yoga or rituals

These smells weren't random—they were used to **elevate consciousness**.
Even your mind responds to them with **silence, stillness, and sharpness**.

> "Where there is sacred scent, there is sacred presence."

🔗 The Secret Power: Smell as a Personal Trigger

You can actually **train your brain** to connect a scent with a certain mental state.

Here's how:

1. Choose a positive scent (essential oil or perfume)
2. Use it only while doing something intentional: journaling, meditating, or studying
3. Repeat this over time

Now your brain forms a shortcut:

> "This smell = this state of mind."

Later, even when you're distracted, just smelling that scent can bring you **back into flow**.

👃 Quick Exercise: Smell Scan

> ✍️ Try this right now:
>
> - What are 3 smells you associate with comfort?

- What is one smell that instantly reminds you of childhood?
- Is there a scent that calms or energizes you?
- Can you add a new scent to your workspace?

This is your **emotional toolkit**—invisible, but powerful.

Quotes You Can Share - #teensimage

- "Your nose remembers what your eyes forget."
- "Smell is the shortcut between memory and emotion."
- "Control your air, and you can control your mood."
- "Every scent carries a story."
- "What you smell creates what you feel—before you can think."

Progress Gauge.

5.

The Skin — The Language of Connection

🧠 Introduction: Skin Feels What Words Can't Express

The skin is the body's **largest organ**, but most people don't realize how deeply it influences their **mind**, **mood**, and **identity**.

We think of touch as just pressure—like a handshake, a pat, or a poke.
But **touch is the first sense you ever felt**, even before you were born.

From the time you're a baby to now as a teen, the skin has been silently recording **safety**, **comfort**, **trauma**, and **trust**.

> "Your skin holds every emotional fingerprint you've ever felt."

🔬 The Science of Skin and Sensation

Your skin contains millions of **nerve endings** that detect:

- **Temperature** (hot/cold)
- **Pressure** (light/heavy)
- **Pain**
- **Vibration**
- **Emotional warmth**

All these signals go straight to the brain's **somatosensory cortex**—and trigger **emotional responses**, not just physical ones.

This is why:

- A warm hug relaxes you.
- A sudden slap shocks you.
- Even a gentle hand on your shoulder can make you cry if you're feeling weak.

Touch doesn't just register on the skin.
It **talks to the heart**.

🧬 Comfort and Connection Through Skin

Your skin is constantly picking up information like:

- Is this person safe?

- Am I loved?
- Do I belong here?
- Should I protect myself?

Even **one moment of positive touch**—like a high-five, a hug from a parent, or a friend's shoulder bump—can release **oxytocin**, the "bonding" hormone.

That's why:

- Babies stop crying when held.
- Athletes perform better after team huddles.
- You feel calm after a good head massage or a back rub.

> "We may speak different languages, but the skin understands them all."

Negative Touch and Emotional Scars

But just like good touch heals—**bad or unwanted touch wounds** deeply.

- A rough push
- An unwanted grip
- Touch that crosses boundaries
- Or even the **absence** of touch (emotional neglect)

All of these can affect:

- Your **self-worth**
- Your **trust in others**
- Your ability to feel **safe in your own body**
- "When the skin is hurt, the heart remembers."

This is why **learning boundaries**—both giving and receiving—is part of shaping your IMAGE.

✋ Touch as a Language

Think of touch like a **silent language**:

Type of Touch	Emotional Meaning
Gentle hug	Safety / Comfort
High-five	Approval / Bonding
Pat on back	Encouragement
Tight grip	Control / Fear
No touch at all	Disconnection / Distance

You don't always need words.
Your **skin feels what your heart knows**.

💡 Two Situations: The Power of Skin

🧍 Situation 1: The Comfort of a Simple Hug

You've had a bad day. Failed a test. Got shouted at.
Your mind is spiraling.

A friend walks up and gives you a **silent 5-second hug**.

No words. No advice.
Just warmth, pressure, presence.

Your brain releases:

- **Oxytocin** (bonding)
- **Dopamine** (motivation)
- **Serotonin** (calm and safety)

You still have problems—but now you're emotionally **strong enough to face them**.

🛏 Situation 2: Feeling Lonely in Your Room

It's late. You're in bed, scrolling endlessly.

You feel disconnected—even though you've been "online" all day.

That's because:

- Your **body hasn't received touch**.
- Your brain is **starved of emotional safety signals**.
- Virtual likes ≠ physical connection.

That's when **a family member's presence, a pet's touch, or even wrapping yourself in a blanket** becomes healing.

The skin remembers **warmth**, not WiFi.

🧘 Touch, Self-Image, and Self-Love

Do you feel **comfortable in your own skin**?

That's not just a saying—it's a state of inner peace.

When you care for your body—clean it, rest it, move it, hydrate it—you're sending a message to your nervous system:

> "I respect myself. I'm safe here."

Practices like:

- **Skin care**
- **Stretching**
- **Massage**
- **Warm showers**
- **Wearing clothes that make you feel good**

...can actually **reprogram your self-worth**, not just your appearance.

Quotes You Can Share - #teensimage

- "Your skin is the boundary between the world and your soul."
- "One touch can say what a thousand words cannot."
- "To be touched with respect is to be reminded you matter."
- "You can't hug through a screen—but your skin still needs it."
- "Healing begins where safe touch returns."

Progress Gauge.

📕 PART 1 SUMMARY

TEENS – Your 5 Portals of Perception

Every second, your senses—**Tongue, Eyes, Ears, Nose, Skin**—are collecting information from the world around you.

That sensory information becomes:

➡ Thoughts
➡ Feelings
➡ Memories
➡ Habits
➡ Your IMAGE (inner and outer)

> 🧠 **"The senses don't just help you survive—they shape who you become."**

🔄 THE TEENS INPUT → IMAGE OUTPUT LOGIC:

Sense	What It Takes In	What It Programs
👅 **Tongue**	Taste & Words	Habits, cravings, discipline, self-talk
👁 **Eyes**	Visuals & Media	Beliefs, body image, comparison
👂 **Ears**	Music & Words	Inner voice, emotions, influence
👃 **Nose**	Scents & Smells	Emotional memories, comfort, mood

🖐 **Skin**	Touch & Sensation	Safety, self-worth, connection

💥 THE CYCLE:

Senses ➜ Brain ➜ Patterns ➜ Reactions ➜ Self-Image ➜ Life Choices

You become a reflection of what your senses are exposed to every day.

> ✨ "You are not just what you think—you are what you've been absorbing."

🔑 YOUR POWER:

You can't always control your environment.
But you can choose what you:

- Taste with intention
- Watch with awareness
- Hear with discernment
- Smell with purpose
- Touch with respect

This awareness is how you build the IMAGE **you** want—not the one the world imposes.

6.

Inner IMAGE vs Outer IMAGE

ThinWhat You k vs What They See

🎯 Why This Chapter Matters

Most people spend their teenage years worrying about how they look, dress, talk, and act in public. That's your **Outer IMAGE**.

But very few realize there's a more powerful force running the show from behind the scenes—your **Inner IMAGE**.

If you want to **look confident**, you must first **feel confident**.
If you want to be **liked**, you must first **like yourself**.
That's the difference between fixing the **mirror**... and actually washing your **face**.

Let's explore both sides.

⭕ Outer IMAGE: What the World Sees

Your Outer IMAGE is how you show up in front of others. It includes:

- Your **clothes** and **style**
- Your **voice** and **tone**
- Your **body language**
- Your **Instagram bio**, profile picture, and posts
- The **vibe** you give off in a group

It's **what others assume about you**—before you even speak.

> "First impressions aren't always true.
> But they're powerful."

Your Outer IMAGE is important because it:

- Influences opportunities
- Affects relationships
- Reflects your current mental state

But the real question is—**who's controlling it?**

🧠 Inner IMAGE: What You Tell Yourself

Your Inner IMAGE is **your belief system**. It's made up of:

- The **self-talk** in your head
- Your **past experiences** and emotional memory
- Your **confidence level**
- The **labels** you've accepted ("I'm shy", "I'm smart", "I'm not good enough")
- Your **vision of who you want to become**

This image is **not seen** by the world—but it drives **every choice you make**.

If your inner image says:

- "I'm not attractive" → You'll avoid attention
- "I'm not smart" → You'll stop trying to learn
- "Nobody listens to me" → You'll stay silent in groups

You can wear branded clothes, get 1,000 likes, or speak English fluently…
But if your **inner voice is negative**, it will pull your outer image down like gravity.

🔄 The Link Between the Two

Think of your Inner and Outer IMAGE like this:

INNER IMAGE 🧠	OUTER IMAGE 🪞
Code	Screen
Root	Fruit
Software	Display
Cause	Effect

When you fix the software, the screen responds.
When you water the root, the fruit becomes sweet.
That's why **true self-improvement starts inside.**

📦 Where Did Your Inner IMAGE Come From?

Remember Part 1?

Your **5 senses** (TEENS) act like **data collectors**.
They take in:

- What people say about you
- How others treat you
- What you hear, see, feel

Over time, these sensory inputs create **emotional impressions**.
Your brain **records them as truth**.

For example:

- If someone always called you "useless" → your inner voice may repeat it

- If a teacher once praised you → that becomes a source of confidence
- If you failed once → your brain might label you a "failure"

But here's the truth:

> "Most of your Inner IMAGE was not chosen by you.
> It was **installed** by your surroundings."

🔓 But You Can Rebuild It

Just like apps can be updated, your Inner IMAGE can be **rewired**.

That's where self-awareness, conscious thinking, and journaling come in (we'll go deeper in upcoming chapters).

> "You're not stuck with the voice in your head—
> You can train it."

🧩 A Simple Real-Life Analogy

You're Going to a School Function

You've dressed well (Outer IMAGE ✔),
But inside, you're nervous: "What if I mess up?" (Inner IMAGE ✖)

People see you, but they **feel your energy**.
Even your smile looks shaky.
Your confidence doesn't match your clothes.

Now flip it:

Same event.
You've practiced, feel prepared, and believe in yourself.
You're still wearing the same outfit—but this time your **posture is different**, your voice is clear, and people notice something real.

That's the power of **alignment**.

🛠 Activity: Mirror Check vs Mind Check

Try this before going out or starting your day:

Check	How to Do It
Mirror Check	Stand in front of the mirror. Is your posture confident? Are you slouching? Are you smiling for real?
Mind Check	Ask: "What am I telling myself today?" Is it empowering or discouraging?

Both are equally important.
Fix the mirror—but **also clean the lens inside your mind.**

📢 Quotes You Can Share - #teensimage

- "Confidence isn't in the clothes—it's in the code."
- "Fix the mirror, yes. But wash your face first."
- "You're not what people say about you. You're what you say when you're alone."
- "The real glow-up is internal."
- "Outer image is a photo. Inner image is the filter."

📶 Progress Gauge.

7.

Habits Are Like Code

You're Programming Yourself Every Day

🧠 Why This Chapter Matters

Every day, you repeat small actions—brushing your teeth, scrolling Instagram, eating certain foods, saying "I'll do it later."

These don't seem like a big deal…

But guess what?

Each of those actions is a **line of code** you're writing into your brain.
And over time, your brain **runs** those codes without even asking you.

> "You are not born with habits.
> You build them.
> And they end up building you."

Let's decode how it works—and how you can become the programmer.

🧩 Habits = Loops Created by Senses

Go back to TEENS—your five senses.

They collect data:
A smell, a sound, a taste, an image, or a touch.

That input **triggers a feeling** → which leads to an action → which gives a reward → and the brain saves that pattern.

Example:
You hear a notification (👂 Ears) → You feel curious → You check the phone → You get a message → Brain says "Nice!"
Next time? Your hand moves automatically.

This is the **Habit Loop**:

🔄 **Cue → Craving → Action → Reward**

- **Cue:** Something triggers your senses
- **Craving:** Your brain wants the feel-good result
- **Action:** You respond (almost without thinking)
- **Reward:** Your brain saves it as "do this again!"

This loop = your brain's **coding system**.

👨‍💻 You Are the Programmer

- Think of your brain as a **computer**.
- Every time you:
- Skip a workout → You code laziness

- Delay homework → You code procrastination
- Watch motivational videos → You code awareness
- Wake up early → You code discipline

And the more times you run that code...
The faster your brain executes it.
That's **neuroplasticity**—the brain's ability to **rewire** based on repetition.

> "Repetition is reputation.
> Do it enough, and it becomes your identity."

🧠 Brain Coding Is Neutral

Your brain doesn't care if the habit is good or bad.
It just cares: *"Have I done this before?"*

So if you...

- Complain daily → Brain makes you a natural complainer
- Read daily → Brain makes you a curious learner
- Lie regularly → Brain removes guilt
- Speak truth often → Brain makes honesty your comfort zone

Your **inputs → become actions → become patterns → become personality**.

💡 Real-Life Analogy: Instagram Algorithm

Instagram doesn't judge what you watch.
It just notices: "You spent 10 sec on this kind of reel? Here's more of that."

Your brain works the same.

Whatever you "watch" or "do" often—your brain says:

> "Let me make this easier next time."

You're basically **training your algorithm**.

So ask:

> "What habits am I reinforcing daily?"
> "What kind of person is this coding me into?"

⚙️ Habit Audit: Install or Uninstall?

Habit	Is it helping?	Keep/Uninstall?
Scrolling before sleep	Sleep worse?	Uninstall ❌
Drinking water after waking	Feel energized?	Keep ✅
Overthinking failure	Makes you afraid?	Uninstall ❌
Journaling emotions	Makes you clear?	Keep ✅

Let's break it down simply. Your brain = your operating system.
Update it like your phone.
Remove bugs, install better versions.

🛠️ How to Code Better Habits (for Teens)

1. **Start Small, Code One Line**
   → Don't try to overhaul everything. Just change one thing consistently.

2. **Link New to Old**
   → Example: After brushing teeth, drink water.
   This connects a new habit to a stable one = "habit stacking."

3. **Visual Reminders Are Code Anchors**
   → A sticky note, wallpaper, or water bottle with a quote acts like a *trigger* for better action.

4. **Reward Yourself Intentionally**
   → Celebrate even small wins. Your brain loves rewards—so use them smartly.

5. **Correct the Bug, Don't Blame the Code**
   → If you fail, don't say "I'm weak." Say, "Okay, what was the trigger?" and fix it.

📢 Quotes You Can Share - #teensimage

- "Your habits write your code.

  Your code writes your life."
- "Repeat anything long enough—it becomes your identity."

- “Your brain is programmable. The question is—who’s doing the programming?”
- “One small act done daily can change your future fully.”
- “You don’t rise to your goals—you fall to your patterns.”

Progress Gauge.

8.

The Science Behind IMAGE

Why You Become What You Repeatedly Sense and Do

🧬 What is IMAGE, Scientifically?

The word IMAGE usually makes people think of selfies, mirrors, or Instagram filters.

But in science, IMAGE stands for:
Integrated Molecular Analysis of Gene Expression
(A complex way of saying: how your genes respond to your environment.)

In this book, IMAGE means:

> "The version of yourself that is created from what your senses absorb and what your brain repeats."

Every day, your **senses (TEENS)** feed your brain thousands of signals.
Your brain converts those signals into **emotions, memories, thoughts, and habits**.

Over time, this process **builds the version of you**—your personal IMAGE.

🧠 Brain + Body = Data Processors

Think of your brain and body like a massive tech system.
Each sense is like a keyboard, mouse, or voice input.

- Tongue (taste & speech)
- Eyes (visual content)
- Ears (sounds, words)
- Nose (smells + emotional memory)
- Skin (touch, temperature, comfort)

Every time you sense something, your brain responds with a chemical reaction:

- See something funny → Brain releases dopamine (pleasure)
- Hear someone insult you → Brain releases cortisol (stress)
- Feel comfort from touch → Brain releases oxytocin (trust)

These **chemical reactions** shape your feelings, and those feelings start building patterns.

🧠 The Brain is Plastic (Neuroplasticity)

Your brain is not fixed like cement—it's plastic.
That means it can **rewire itself** based on what you do again and again.

This is called **neuroplasticity**.

So, when you:

- Complain every day → Brain builds "complain highways"
- Practice gratitude daily → Brain builds "positive thought highways"
- Keep checking your phone → Brain makes it automatic

> "Your brain doesn't care what you repeat—it just gets better at it."

Teens have **super-high neuroplasticity**, which means:
You're in the most powerful coding phase of your life.

🧬 Epigenetics: How Habits Shape Your Biology

You don't just inherit genes from your parents
You also inherit a **switchboard** that decides which genes turn **ON** or **OFF**.

That switchboard is influenced by:

- Environment
- Emotions
- Diet

- Sleep
- Repeated behaviors

This science is called **epigenetics**.

So when you repeatedly choose poor habits, you can activate genes linked to:

- Anxiety
- Inflammation
- Low energy

But when you choose better inputs and routines, you activate genes for:

- Calmness
- Strength
- Focus

> You are not just reacting to life.
> You are biologically shaping your future—one action at a time.

Mirror Neurons: How You Copy What You Sense

You've seen this before:

- You yawn because someone else yawned.
- You feel sad during a movie—even though it's fiction.
- You mimic your favorite influencer's hand gestures or slang.

This happens because of **mirror neurons** in your brain.
They light up when you **watch someone else doing something**—as if *you're doing it too.*

So, if your senses are always exposed to:

- Anger → You pick up irritability
- Drama → You become reactive
- Peaceful content → You build patience
- Confident people → You absorb confidence

> What you watch, you become.
> Who you listen to, you echo.

This is how your **outer world becomes your inner world**—and shapes your IMAGE.

The Invisible Sculptor: Your Senses

You can't always see it, but your **TEENS (5 senses)** are constantly sculpting your IMAGE.

They're like invisible chisels:

- **Your tongue** sculpts habits and confidence (food + speech)
- **Your eyes** shape perception and self-image (what you see daily)
- **Your ears** influence beliefs and decisions (music, voices, opinions)
- **Your nose** triggers memories and comfort zones (smells + emotions)
- **Your skin** teaches you safety, love, or fear (touch + temperature)

Together, they **code who you're becoming** every day.

✨ Realization: You Are the Coder

This chapter isn't just about science.
It's a **wake-up call**:

You're not helpless.
You're programmable.
And better—**you are the programmer**.

Ask yourself:

- "What am I letting into my system?"
- "Which habits am I repeating unconsciously?"

- “What version of myself am I building?”

Because the science is clear:

> “What you repeat gets stronger.
> What you sense becomes your self.
> What you believe becomes your brain’s truth.”

📢 Quotes You Can Share - #teensimage

- “Your IMAGE isn’t fixed. It’s coded—by your senses, your habits, and your choices.”
- “You’re not just shaped by genes. You’re shaped by what you repeat.”
- “Your brain will become whatever you train it to become.”
- “You can’t control your genes, but you can control their triggers.”
- “You are not just becoming older. You are becoming programmed.”

📶 Progress Gauge.

📕 PART 2 SUMMARY

From Unconscious Input to Conscious Programming

🔍 WHY THIS PART MATTERS:

Your senses are constantly feeding your brain.
But now, it's time to decide what you **want to become**.
This part shows you how to build your IMAGE—from the **inside out**.

🧠 Chapter 6: Inner IMAGE vs Outer IMAGE

"Confidence isn't in the clothes—it's in the code."

- **Outer IMAGE** = What people see (style, posture, posts)
- **Inner IMAGE** = What you tell yourself when you're alone (self-talk, beliefs, emotional memory)
- If your inner image is broken, your outer one will eventually crack—even if it looks perfect.
- Your inner image was **installed by your surroundings**, but now **you can rebuild it**.

🔁 **Key Metaphors**: Software → Display, Root → Fruit
🛠 **Tools**: Mirror Check + Mind Check
💬 **Quote**: *"Fix the mirror, yes. But wash your face first."*

👨‍💻 Chapter 7: Habits Are Like Code

> *"You are not born with habits. You build them. And they build you."*

- Habits are created through **sensory loops**:
  - **Cue → Craving → Action → Reward**
- Your brain is like a computer—it runs whatever you repeat.
- You can program it with discipline, curiosity, laziness, or procrastination.
- **Neuroplasticity** means your brain gets better at whatever you do often.

🧠 **Analogy**: Instagram algorithm = Your mind. What you engage with, it gives more of.
🛠 **Tools**: Habit Audit, Habit Stacking, Visual Reminders
💬 **Quote**: *"Your brain is programmable. The question is—who's doing the programming?"*

🧬 Chapter 8: The Science Behind IMAGE

> *"What you repeat gets stronger. What you sense becomes your self."*

- Scientific IMAGE = how your **genes express** based on your environment
- **TEENS inputs** trigger hormones and emotions → become habits → shape your personality

- Your brain is **plastic** (can rewire) and your genes are **programmable** (epigenetics)
- **Mirror neurons** copy what you see, feel, hear—so choose your environment carefully

🧠 **Key Concepts**: Neuroplasticity, Epigenetics, Mirror Neurons
🧊 **Analogy**: Senses = Invisible Sculptors of your IMAGE
💬 **Quote**: *"You're not just becoming older. You're becoming programmed."*

🔑 PART 2 CORE MESSAGE:

You are the coder of your future.
You can't always control what you inherited.
But you can **control what you install, repeat, and believe**.

⚙️ LOGIC FLOW OF PART 2:

Senses → Beliefs → Habits → Patterns → IMAGE → Identity → Life

9.

Sense-Check Audit Activity

"You can't control your IMAGE if you don't observe it."

🔍 Why This Chapter Matters

Every day, your senses are receiving information—sometimes helpful, sometimes harmful.

The problem?
You don't even notice it happening.
Your brain is recording everything:
👁 What you see.
👂 What you hear.
👅 What you eat and say.
👃 What you smell.
✋ What you touch and feel.

This quiet intake becomes your **daily data**. And just like code in a program, this data shapes how you **think, feel, act, and react**.

So if you want to change your life, change your IMAGE, or break a negative loop—you first need to **see the pattern**.

That's what this chapter helps you do.

🎯 What You'll Learn in This Chapter

- How to **observe your daily sensory inputs**
- How to reflect: Is this helping or harming my IMAGE?
- How to spot patterns you didn't even know existed
- How to build a system of **self-awareness** that becomes automatic over time

---

🔁 The TEENS Sense-Check System

Use this daily or weekly. It's simple.
All you need is a few minutes and a notebook (or your phone notes).

👅 T — Tongue: What You Eat and Speak

- What food did I eat today? Was it helping or harming my energy?
- Did I eat because of real hunger—or just boredom/craving?
- What kind of **words** did I speak today?

- Uplifting or complaining?
- Truthful or exaggerated?
- Loving or rude?

☑ Check-In Example:

Breakfast: Ate junk in a hurry
Lunch: Healthy but skipped protein
Spoke harshly during school argument
Complimented friend = felt good

👁 E — Eyes: What You Saw

- What kind of **visual content** did I watch today?
- Social media, TV, YouTube, posters, ads
- Did it inspire me or drain me?
- Did I compare myself to others online?

☑ Check-In Example:

Scrolled 2 hours on Instagram
Saw one video that made me feel insecure
Saw a motivational clip that I saved and rewatched

👂 E — Ears: What You Heard

- What music or voices did I listen to?

- What kind of tone did I speak in or hear from others?
    - Gossip? Kindness? Sarcasm? Inspiration?
- What was the **loudest voice in my head** today?

✅ Check-In Example:

Heard teacher yell—felt anxious
Listened to calming music in evening
My own thoughts were very negative during lunch

👃 N — Nose: What You Smelled

- Did I smell something that triggered a memory?
- What scents made me feel calm or alert?
- Did any smell feel unpleasant or overwhelming?

✅ Check-In Example:

Smelled perfume from a classmate—reminded me of mom
Walked past garbage—felt disgusted
Lit a candle at home and felt peaceful

✋ S — Skin: What You Touched and Felt

- Did I feel comforted today? Hugs, handshake, physical safety?
- Was I exposed to too much heat/cold/uncomfortable clothing?

- How did physical sensation affect my **mood or energy**?

✅ Check-In Example:

> Felt calm when I hugged my pet
> Wore tight shoes—felt irritated in class
> Skin felt dry and itchy = low focus

🧠 Bonus Layer: Emotional Mapping

After your TEENS check-in, ask:

> "What emotion showed up the most today?"
> 😊 Joy
> 😒 Boredom
> 😠 Anger
> 😨 Anxiety
> 😍 Love
> 😞 Guilt
> 😌 Calm

Then link it to a sense.
For example:

- Angry because I heard shouting (👂)
- Calm after warm bath (✋)
- Anxious after scrolling dark videos (👁)

📊 Weekly Pattern Tracker (Sample Table)

Sense	Positive Input	Negative Input	Noticed Pattern
Tongue	Healthy breakfast	Late-night chips	Crave sugar when stressed
Eyes	Watched TED Talk	Compared body on IG	IG = mood drops
Ears	Uplifting music	Gossip at lunch	Feel drained after gossip
Nose	Lavender oil	None	Calms me before study
Skin	Cozy hoodie	Uncomfortabl e bench	Hard chairs = low focus

---

🗣 A Simple Realization

> "Wow—I never noticed that I snack more when I watch YouTube."
> "I always get angry after hearing certain people talk."
> "Good music boosts my confidence more than I thought."

This is the moment of power.
Because what you observe—you can change.
What you're unaware of—controls you.

✅ Your Mission Today

Take 15 minutes.
Use the Sense-Check template above.
Write what you experienced through TEENS.
Highlight any aha-moments, triggers, or patterns.

🧠 The goal is not to be perfect—it's to be **present**.

📢 Quotes You Can Share - #teensimage

- "What you don't observe is already shaping you."
- "You're not just scrolling—you're coding your brain."
- "Tiny triggers create major moods—track them."
- "Your IMAGE isn't built in a day. It's built every day."
- "You can't upgrade your life with outdated inputs."

📶 Progress Gauge.

10.

Reflection Exercises — Journaling Your IMAGE

"If you can write it, you can rewrite it."

🔎 Why Reflection Matters

Let's get real.

You've gone through your daily sense-check.
You've noticed what enters through your **TEENS** (Tongue, Eyes, Ears, Nose, Skin).
Now comes the deeper part: **understanding what it's doing to you inside.**

Think of this chapter like holding up a mirror—not to your face, but to your **thoughts, emotions, and patterns**.

Because whatever IMAGE you're expressing on the outside…
Started as something **coded inside** you.

Reflection = the moment where your **internal coding becomes visible**.

And guess what?

If you can see it,
You can **shift it.**

🧠 What You'll Learn in This Chapter

- How to journal with **purpose and clarity**
- Identify your **emotional triggers and repetitive reactions**
- Catch the **inner story** that's shaping your self-image
- Start reprogramming old beliefs using your own words

📓 1. The Self-Scan Technique (5-Minute Daily Journal)

Here's a **simple daily structure** you can use every evening:

✍️ Step 1: What happened today?

- List 2–3 key events or moments.
- Example:
  "Argued with a friend."
  "Got complimented on my outfit."
  "Skipped study for reels again."

✍️ Step 2: What did I feel?

- Identify the emotion in that moment.
- Angry? Embarrassed? Proud? Ashamed? Confused? Energized?

Step 3: What triggered that emotion?

- Was it something you **saw**, **heard**, **felt**, **ate**, or **smelled**?
- Was it from inside (thoughts) or outside (people/environment)?

Step 4: What did I tell myself after it happened?

- "I always mess up."
- "Nobody understands me."
- "I deserve to relax."
- "I handled that like a boss."

This is the line that shapes your inner IMAGE.

---

2. Reflection Prompts: Weekly Deep Dive

Each week, take 20–30 minutes to reflect using these:

Pattern Discovery

- What situations trigger me again and again?

- Do I avoid certain feelings or people often?
- What do I always crave when I feel stressed?
- Is my IMAGE built more on reaction or intention?

🎭 Outer vs. Inner Self

- What IMAGE do I try to show others?
- Does it match how I truly feel inside?
- Where am I pretending or performing?
- What part of me do I hide?

💬 Self-Talk Audit

- What do I say to myself when I fail?
- What's one harsh sentence I repeat internally?
- What's one kind phrase I rarely say to myself?

📈 Growth Check

- What positive habit am I proud of this week?

- When did I handle a trigger better than before?
- What am I learning about myself through journaling?

🧩 Real Example: Sneha's Journal (Age 16)

📅 Tuesday

1. Didn't answer in class even though I knew the answer.
2. Felt small and nervous.
3. Triggered by classmates who laughed yesterday.
4. Inner thought: "Don't risk it. They'll judge again."
5. Realization: I'm letting **yesterday's input** shape today's self-image.

✨ Rewriting That Inner Script

Here's the most powerful part:

Every time you **catch** a limiting belief or painful memory—
You have a chance to **rewrite it.**

Ask:

> "Is this belief still useful?"
> "Who taught me this story?"
> "What truth would I rather live by?"

Then create a new line:

> "I may be judged, but I won't shrink."
> "I'm not my past reaction—I'm my present choice."
> "Confidence grows one step at a time."

You're not lying to yourself.
You're choosing a **healthier internal language.**

📓 Create Your Journal Code Page

At the end of this chapter, reserve a page for your:

- Most common **emotions**
- Repetitive **trigger points**
- Negative **self-talk lines**
- Your NEW **affirmations or self-guiding phrases**

This becomes your **personal decoding map.**

🔁 Practice Makes Permanent

Reflection isn't about becoming perfect.
It's about becoming **aware**.

The more often you journal,
The more clearly you'll see how your **TEENS inputs** → form your emotional life → and shape your **self-image**.

And once you're aware,
You're no longer running an old script.
You're the one writing the code.

📢 Quotes You Can Share - #teensimage

- "If you can write it, you can rewrite it."
- "Self-awareness isn't a skill—it's a superpower."
- "The story you tell yourself becomes the life you live."
- "Your triggers are not the problem—your reactions are the code."
- "Journaling is how you talk to the future version of yourself."

📶 Progress Gauge.

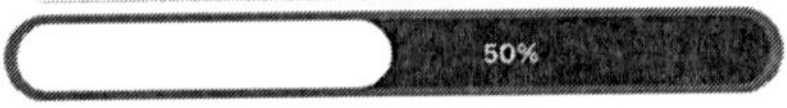

11.

Visualization & Reprogramming

"You become what you mentally rehearse."

🔁 Why Reprogramming Is Needed

By now, you've seen your patterns.
Through **sense-checks** and **reflection journaling**, you've spotted:

- Repetitive emotional triggers
- Negative self-talk loops
- Old beliefs that no longer help you

But here's the truth:
Awareness alone isn't enough.

You need a way to **change the inner code**.
To replace what's not serving you,
with what supports your growth.

That's where **visualization** comes in.

🧠 The Science of Mental Rehearsal

Your brain doesn't fully know the difference between:

- something you actually do
- and something you vividly imagine doing

This is called **neuroplasticity**—your brain rewiring itself through repeated thought.

Olympic athletes, CEOs, musicians, and spiritual seekers all use this same tool:

> ✨ They visualize their best self performing the way they want—until it becomes natural.

You can do the same.

👁 What Is Visualization?

Visualization is the practice of **mentally picturing** a desired outcome or experience.
Not just seeing it like a movie,
but **feeling it**—as if it's happening now.

It works because your brain treats imagined events as real **training.**

> If journaling is diagnosis,
> **Visualization is a prescription.**

✨ The Reprogramming Formula

Here's a simple step-by-step process to start changing your inner image.

🎧 Step 1: Find a Quiet Space (2–5 mins)

- Sit or lie down with spine straight
- Close your eyes
- Take 5 deep breaths to relax your body and center your attention

---

🎯 Step 2: Bring Up an Old Pattern

Pick a habit, trigger, or moment you want to shift.
Example:

- "I always freeze when it's my turn to speak."
- "I scroll endlessly when I'm stressed."
- "I feel invisible in group conversations."

🎥 Step 3: Create the New Mental Scene

Now imagine the **same situation**…
But this time, you **respond differently**:

- You speak up with calm confidence.
- You pause, breathe, and close your phone.
- You smile, make eye contact, and express your view.

Visualize every detail:

- How you stand
- What you're wearing
- The expressions on others' faces
- The feeling in your body

Most important:
Feel the energy of success—peace, confidence, clarity.

🔁 Step 4: Repeat That Scene Daily

Practice this new version of you **every day for 7–21 days**.
Why?

Because repetition = rewiring.
You're literally training your brain to behave from a different emotional base.

The more often you **see it** and **feel it**,
the more likely your body will **live it**.

💡 Quick Tip: Link Visualization to a Real Habit

Example:

- Visualize right after brushing your teeth
- Or right before bed
- Or during your commute/walk

This makes it easier to stick with.

🗣️ Add Affirmations to Strengthen It

While visualizing, say positive affirmations aloud or in your mind:

- "I speak with clarity and courage."
- "I pause before reacting."
- "I choose what supports my growth."
- "I don't chase—I attract by being me."

These **verbal codes** reinforce the visual scene.

🧘 Try This: 1-Minute Power Script

Here's a mini mental script to start with:

I see myself calm and aware.
I handle pressure with peace.
When I speak, people listen.
I no longer shrink—I expand into who I really am.
I choose actions that support my IMAGE.

Repeat this after journaling—or before facing a challenge.

💻 Real-Life Parallel: Programming a Device

Imagine your brain is a smartphone.
Over the years, it's downloaded **apps** (beliefs) from:

- parents
- media
- school
- society
- pain

Some of those apps are full of **bugs**.
They drain your battery.
Slow your system.
Crash under pressure.

Visualization is like **deleting the old app and installing a better version**.

You're not faking it.
You're **upgrading your system** to match your highest potential.

👣 Start Small, Stay Consistent

You don't need to visualize for hours.
Even **2–5 minutes a day** works if you do it consistently.

> Think of it like brushing your internal IMAGE.
> Just like outer hygiene, your **inner self** needs daily maintenance too.

✨ Final Message: You're Already the Person You Want to Be

The version of you who is focused, confident, kind, disciplined—that version is **already inside you.**

You don't have to find it.
You just have to **remove the dust** of fear, doubt, and old programming.

And each time you visualize…
You're clearing that dust,
and letting your **true IMAGE** shine through.

📢 Quotes You Can Share - #teensimage

1. “You become what you mentally rehearse.”

2. “Visualization is not daydreaming. It’s training.”

3. “Your brain is a device. Reprogram it before it crashes on old beliefs.”

4. “What you repeat, you rewire.”

5. “Your best self isn’t lost. It’s just buried under dust. Visualize—and wipe it clean.”

📶 Progress Gauge.

12.

Choosing Your Influences

"You become the environment you live in—inside and out."

Why Influences Matter

Look around you.

Now look within you.

The people you talk to, the reels you scroll, the music you play, the rooms you sit in, the words you hear daily…

All of these things are not just passing moments—they are **inputs.**
And what do inputs do?

> They shape your IMAGE.
> They become your thoughts.
> They define your desires.
> They decide your direction.

Your IMAGE isn't just a **personal effort**.
It's a **shared construction.**
The question is:

> Are you **choosing** your influences…
> Or just letting them choose you?

🧪 The Influence Equation

Let's simplify it:

Input → Emotion → Habit → Identity

Every influence you allow becomes an input.
That input triggers an emotion.
That emotion drives a habit.
That habit creates your personality (and eventually your destiny).

> **Your surroundings aren't neutral.**
> They are programming you, even in silence.

🧭 Three Circles of Influence

Visualize your life as three **concentric circles**:

1️⃣ Inner Circle – People Closest to You

- Friends
- Family
- Mentors
- Classmates / teammates

Ask: Do they inspire growth or drain your energy?

2️⃣ Middle Circle – Daily Environments

- School / coaching centers
- Home atmosphere
- Social media feeds
- YouTube, music, books

Ask: What are these spaces teaching me?

3 Outer Circle – Culture & Trends

- Celebrities, influencers
- Society's definitions of success
- News, memes, viral content

Ask: What values am I absorbing without even noticing?

Realize: You're Always Being Influenced

Whether you notice or not, something is always entering your subconscious.

- A sarcastic reel may plant self-doubt.
- A positive quote may unlock strength.
- A chill song might relax you—or reinforce laziness.

- A friend's anxiety may transfer to you.

Silence is not safety.
Absence of choice is still a choice.

So let's make it **conscious.**

🔍 Influence Audit Activity

Grab your journal and answer honestly:

👥 People

- Who makes me feel **more myself**?
- Who brings out my worst habits?
- Who gives energy vs. who takes it?
- Who listens with presence?
- Who do I admire—and why?

📱 Digital

- What kind of content fills my feed?
- How do I feel after 30 mins of scrolling?
- Which apps bring inspiration vs. distraction?
- Who do I follow out of **habit**, not **intention**?

🧠 Beliefs

- Which messages do I hear often? ("Be rich or you're a loser", "Be cool over kind", "Success = attention")
- Are these messages even **true**?
- Who benefits if I keep believing them?

🔄 Replace Unconscious with Conscious Inputs

You can't always control your environment.
But you can control what you **feed your IMAGE** with.

Here's how to start:

✅ Start Choosing Your Circle

- Spend more time with those who uplift you
- Have **one honest conversation** a week with someone wiser
- Build a "Growth Group" of 2–3 friends who reflect and level up with you

---

✅ Curate Your Digital Diet

- Follow 5 pages that teach you, uplift you, or challenge your thinking

- Unfollow one toxic account each week
- Limit doomscrolling—replace with an audiobook, podcast, or note-taking

📱 Try this mantra:
"If it's not helping me grow, it's got to go."

✅ **Redesign Your Spaces**

- Clean your room = Clear your mind
- Add a "focus corner" in your space for reflection or study
- Put visual cues: affirmation cards, inspiring quotes, calming colors

---

🔥 Real Story: Devesh's Turnaround

Devesh was smart, but constantly anxious and unmotivated.
He realized his room was always messy, his friends just gossiped, and his feed was filled with FOMO, flex, and memes.
One week, he decided to detox—
Cleared his digital space.
Had tough conversations.
Joined a coding group.
Started journaling.
In 30 days, his mind felt clearer.
His confidence returned—not because he changed, but because his **inputs did.**

🧠 Rewire This Thought:

> ❌ "I can't focus. I'm just lazy."
> ✅ "Maybe I'm not lazy—maybe I'm surrounded by distractions."

You're not broken.
Your IMAGE just needs better lighting.

🌱 Final Message: Protect Your Inner Garden

Imagine your mind is a **garden.**
Your senses are the **gates**.
The people and content around you are **seeds.**

Will you allow Unwanted plants to grow just because they're trending?

Or will you **plant with intention**?

> You don't have to shut out the world.
> You just need to **filter what enters**—
> So your IMAGE grows with purpose.

📢 Quotes You Can Share - #teensimage

- "If it's not helping you grow, it's got to go."
- "Your mind is a garden. Protect the gates."
- "You don't have to block the world—just filter what enters."

- "You are always under the influence. Choose your dose wisely."
- "You're not lazy—you might just be surrounded by distractions."
- "The content you consume today becomes the mindset you wear tomorrow."

Progress Gauge.

13.

Reprogramming Negative Patterns

"You can't delete your past, but you can rewrite your response."

💣 Why Negative Patterns Are So Hard to Break

You've reflected.
You've visualized.
You've started choosing better influences.

But somehow, certain **old patterns** still show up.

- You overthink even when you know better
- You lash out, then regret it
- You feel stuck in a loop—again

Why?

Because many patterns are not just thoughts—they're **emotional imprints** wired into your body and nervous system.

🔁 What gets repeated, gets remembered.
🧠 What gets remembered, gets reinforced.
💥 What gets triggered, gets expressed.

Unless you **break the loop**, the loop becomes you.

🧬 The Science of Pattern Formation

Your brain is a prediction machine.

It hates uncertainty.
So it creates **shortcuts** based on past experience.

- Got ignored once? Now you expect rejection.
- Failed once? Now you avoid trying.
- Criticized for being loud? Now you play small.

These responses become automatic.
They are not you—but they live inside you like emotional code.

> **Negative patterns are not personality—they're programming.**

And any program can be reprogrammed.

🧩 Step 1: Spot the Trigger Loop

Every pattern has 3 parts:

1. **Trigger** – Something happens

2. **Emotion** – You feel a certain way

3. **Reaction** – You respond without thinking

Example:

- Trigger: You're not invited
- Emotion: Unwanted, sad
- Reaction: You isolate or act "cool" to hide the hurt

📝 Write down a recent moment where this happened.
Then break it into:
Trigger → Emotion → Reaction

This helps you see the loop clearly, like debugging a piece of code.

🧠 Step 2: Interrupt the Reaction

Here's the trick: **Don't fight the emotion—interrupt the reaction.**

Try this:

- Pause and name the feeling:
  "I'm feeling rejected right now."
- Take 3 deep breaths
- Use a body anchor: Place your hand on your chest or belly
- Remind yourself:
  "This is a feeling, not a fact."

When you interrupt the automatic reaction, you **create space**— and in that space, you get back your **choice**.

🧰 Step 3: Replace the Old Code

Once you've created space, insert a new pattern.

Let's say your old loop was:

> "I mess up → I panic → I quit"

Replace it with:

> "I mess up → I breathe → I ask what I can learn → I move on"

🧠 Pro tip: Write your **new pattern** in your journal like a script.

Repeat it to yourself.
Visualize it in action.
Feel it until it becomes natural.

This is real reprogramming.

🧘 The Emotional Reset Practice (5 Minutes Daily)

Use this practice to rewire your response pattern:

1. Sit with eyes closed

2. Recall a recent negative pattern

3. Replay it mentally—but now pause at the emotional peak

4. Breathe

5. Choose a new response
6. Visualize yourself handling it better
7. End by saying:
   "I choose peace over pattern."

🚪 Optional Practice: The Door Technique

Imagine a door in your mind labeled "OLD PATTERNS."

Each time you catch yourself falling into the loop, mentally:

- Close that door
- Say: "Not this time."
- Open the next door labeled "GROWTH"
- Step through into your new response

This imagery helps your brain separate **past wiring from present will.**

🎯 Replace These Thought Loops

Here are common toxic thoughts—and their reprogrammed versions:

Old Thought	New Thought
"I'm not good enough"	"I'm improving daily"
"They're better than me"	"I learn from others, not compete with them"
"I always ruin it"	"Every mistake teaches me something valuable"
"They'll leave me"	"The right people stay when I'm real"

Repeat your new thought **even if it feels fake**.
Because fake thoughts repeatedly become **real beliefs**.

🧠 Reframe Failure

❌ "I failed, so I'm a failure."
✅ "I failed, so I'm one step wiser."

Your negative patterns may have helped you **survive** once.
Now it's time to help yourself **grow**.

Honor the past—but don't let it hold the pen.
It's your story.
You decide what gets rewritten.

🔮 Final Message: You Are Not Your Past

Patterns may live in your body—but they are not your soul.

You are not your mistakes.
You are not your worst moment.

You are not your childhood wounds.
You are not what others made you believe.

You are the **one who observes the patterns**—and chooses again.

That's real freedom.
That's real IMAGE power.

Quotes You Can Share - #teensimage

- "You can't delete your past, but you can rewrite your response."
- "Old reactions are not your destiny—they're just unedited code."
- "You are not your triggers. You are the one who responds."
- "Every time you pause, you reclaim your power."
- "Patterns live in the body. But choice lives in the now."

Progress Gauge.

📕 PART 3 SUMMARY

Shaping Your Positive IMAGE

"Observe. Reflect. Visualize. Choose. Reprogram."

Now that you understand how your IMAGE is formed and how habits code your brain, it's time to take charge.
Part 3 gives you the tools to **become the programmer** of your own life.

🔁 Step-by-Step Growth Journey:

1️⃣ Sense-Check Audit (Chapter 9)

- "You can't control your IMAGE if you don't observe it."
- Use the **TEENS system** (Tongue, Eyes, Ears, Nose, Skin) to track your daily inputs.
- Ask: "Is this helping or harming my mood, energy, or thoughts?"
- Discover unconscious patterns that shape how you feel and behave.

🧠 Bonus Tool: Emotional Mapping
📊 Tool: Weekly Pattern Tracker

---

2 Reflection Exercises (Chapter 10)

"If you can write it, you can rewrite it."

- Journal your thoughts, emotions, and triggers with the **Self-Scan Technique**.
- Find the link between your sensory inputs and your emotional reactions.
- Catch old thought loops and begin rewriting your **inner script**.

Tools:

- Weekly Reflection Prompts
- Self-Talk Audit
- Create Your "Journal Code Page"

---

3 Visualization & Reprogramming (Chapter 11)

"You become what you mentally rehearse."

- Use **mental rehearsal** to train your brain to respond with confidence, calm, and clarity.
- Picture the better version of yourself **as if it's real.**
- Reinforce this with **affirmations** and repeat daily.

🧠 Key Science: Neuroplasticity = Your brain changes with repetition
🧘 Practice: 5-minute Visualization Routine + Affirmation Script

---

4️⃣ Choosing Your Influences (Chapter 12)

"You become the environment you live in—inside and out."

- Your friends, feeds, and spaces are shaping your thoughts daily.
- Do an **Influence Audit** to check who and what is helping or hurting your growth.
- Start **curating your circle, your content, and your physical environment.**

🧭 Tool: 3 Circles of Influence
📱 Mantra: "If it's not helping me grow, it's got to go."

5️⃣ Reprogramming Negative Patterns (Chapter 13)

"You can't delete your past—but you can rewrite your response."

- Understand your **emotional loop**: Trigger → Emotion → Reaction.
- Learn how to **interrupt the pattern** and insert a better response.

- Practice visualization, affirmations, and the **Door Technique** to build new reactions.

💼 Tools:

- Emotional Reset Practice
- Reframed Thought List
- "New Code" Journal Prompts

🎯 Wrap-up Part 3: Shaping Your Positive IMAGE

Let's recap how far you've come:

- You audited your senses (Chapter 9)
- You reflected deeply (Chapter 10)
- You visualized a better you (Chapter 11)
- You curated your world (Chapter 12)
- You reprogrammed your loops (Chapter 13)

You've now built the base for a **powerful, conscious IMAGE**—inside and out.

🔑 FINAL MESSAGE:

You're not stuck. You're just coded—and now, you're the coder.

You've:

- Observed your inputs 👀
- Reflected on your patterns 🧠
- Visualized a better you 🎥
- Chosen your influences 🎯
- Rewired your reactions 🔄

That's how you shape a **Positive IMAGE**—not by being perfect, but by being present and intentional.

14.

TEENS IMAGE at School

Your Identity in the Classroom

🎒 Introduction: More Than Just Marks

"Who am I at school?"

Sounds simple—but it's not.
Are you the backbencher? The topper? The one who never answers questions? Or the one who makes everyone laugh?

Without realizing it, school becomes the first stage where your **IMAGE** gets tested and shaped.

And here's the truth:
School doesn't just test your knowledge.
It tests your **nerves, confidence, focus, voice, attention, habits**—everything connected to your **five senses**.

🧠 The Sensory Classroom

School is a **sensory battlefield**.

- **Ears**: The tone of your teacher, classmates whispering, someone mocking your answer
- **Eyes**: Looking at the board, comparing your test score to others, seeing everyone's faces during a presentation
- **Skin**: The comfort of your seat, the nervous sweat during exams
- **Nose**: Smells from the canteen, or someone's perfume triggering a memory
- **Tongue**: Eating junk food before class, or struggling to answer a question out loud

All these small moments enter your **Perceiving Mind** and **start building your Inner Image**—how you see yourself as a student, a friend, a person.

🐻 Peer Pressure and Performance

Let's say:

- You scored low on a test
- Your friend topped it
- Everyone says, "He's the smart one"
- You stop trying because you think, "What's the point?"

❗ That's how academic identity gets limited.

But here's the twist:
It's not your **marks** that define your image.
It's your **reaction** to those marks that does.

Your brain creates a belief from that moment—and if you don't challenge it, it becomes part of your **permanent IMAGE code**.

🧩 Two Kinds of Students: Same Class, Different Worlds

🎓 Student A: "I'm bad at math."

- Based on one failed test
- Avoids math homework
- Shuts down when teacher asks questions
- Builds fear into his academic identity

🎓 Student B: "I didn't understand this chapter."

- Also failed
- Asks for help or watches a video tutorial
- Practices instead of panicking
- Builds growth into his academic identity

The experience is the same.
The **interpretation** is different.
And that difference shapes their future.

👁‍🗨 Sense-Check: How School Shapes Your Inner Dialogue

Ask yourself:

- What kind of **input** am I getting daily at school?
- Who affects my self-image the most? Teachers, friends, toppers, bullies?
- What kind of **self-talk** runs in my head before a test?
- When I speak in class, how do I feel?

These tiny questions expose **huge patterns**.

🧠 TEENS IMAGE Reflection: School & Inner Self

Your school life isn't just about subjects.

It's a lab for:

- **Self-expression** (Tongue)
- **Focus** (Eyes)
- **Listening** (Ears)
- **Energy awareness** (Skin)
- **Reactions** (Nose, instincts)

If you improve how you **use your senses**, you change how you **use your school life**—not just survive it, but shape it into something useful.

🔍 Real-Life Situation

Situation: Teacher calls your name to solve a math problem.

- Your **ears** hear your name.
- Your **tongue** freezes.
- Your **eyes** scan everyone staring.
- Your **skin** sweats.
- Your **inner voice** says: "What if I mess up?"

But what if you've trained your **inner IMAGE** like this:

> "I may not know it yet. But I'm not afraid to try."

Suddenly, you speak anyway.
You don't need to be perfect—you just need to show up.

✏️ Activity: School Self vs Home Self

Write down two versions of yourself:

1. **School Self** – How do you act, feel, and express yourself at school?
2. **Home Self** – How are you different when no one is watching?

Now reflect:

- Why are they different?
- Which one feels more real?
- How can you carry the **real you** into your school life?

🧩 3 Quick Practices to Try This Week

1. **1-Minute Calm**: Before class, close your eyes for 60 seconds and check how you feel. Breathe. Reset.
2. **One Brave Action**: Raise your hand, ask a doubt, or help a friend struggling with a topic.
3. **3-Second Rule**: Before reacting to a class insult or failure, pause for 3 seconds. Respond, don't react.

📢 Quotes You Can Share - #teensimage

- 🎯 "School doesn't build your IMAGE. You do—class by class, thought by thought."
- 🎯 "You're not just learning math or history—you're learning how to respond, reflect, and rise."
- 🎯 "Your rank is temporary. Your reaction becomes your reality."

📶 Progress Gauge.

15.

Social Media & Digital Persona

Filters, Followers & the Fight for the Real You

🎭 Introduction: You Have Two Profiles

Let's be honest.
You have **two versions** of yourself:

- The Real You: The one who feels, fails, learns, and grows.
- The Online You: The one who smiles in perfect lighting, types deep captions, or scrolls silently for hours.

Welcome to your **Digital Persona**—a version of your IMAGE that's shaped not by mirrors, but by **screens**.

👁 Your Eyes Are Online 6–8 Hours a Day

That's not just screen time—that's **sensory input time**.
Every reel, story, post, meme, or DM…

- Sends signals to your **perceiving mind**
- Shapes your **emotions**
- Builds your **inner beliefs**
- Alters your **outer behavior**

You may think you're just "chilling."
But your **IMAGE is downloading data**—one swipe at a time.

🧪 Filters vs. Reality

Think about this:

- A selfie with no filter gets 37 likes
- A filtered photo gets 154 likes
- You start thinking: "Maybe I look better with this filter."

That's where it begins.

You didn't plan to doubt yourself.
But the **dopamine** from more likes becomes a habit.
And now—without realizing—it's harder to post the **real you.**

🧠 How Social Media Hacks Your Brain

Let's decode the science:

- You post → You wait → You get likes → You feel good → You repeat
- Your brain connects “approval” with “performance”
- And slowly, the **need for validation** grows

This creates a dangerous loop:

> Post what gets approved, not what’s authentic.
> Show what looks good, not what feels right.

🔊 How the Senses Are Manipulated

Let’s connect TEENS here:

Sense	Social Media Example	Impact on IMAGE
👁 Eyes	Perfect bodies, curated feeds	You compare yourself
👂 Ears	Trends, gossip, toxic audios	You imitate without thinking
👃 Nose	Smell missing—but triggers memory when offline	Real world feels dull
👅 Tongue	Crave food you saw online	Eating becomes impulsive
👐 Skin	No physical touch	Loneliness hides behind hearts & shares

You're living a **sensory imbalance**—where your mind is overstimulated but your body is untouched.

🔄 Double-Tap vs Deep Identity

Ask yourself:

- Do I post what's true to me—or what fits the trend?
- Do I feel good after scrolling? Or drained?
- Do I control my content—or is it controlling me?

You don't need to quit social media.
You need to **consciously design** your digital IMAGE.

🔒 How to Protect Your Digital Self

Here are **5 Digital Boundaries** every teen should try:

1. **Limit Passive Scrolling**
   – Set a timer. 30 minutes of intentional use is better than 3 hours of passive doomscrolling.
2. **Filter Your Feed Like a Mind Diet**
   – Unfollow accounts that make you feel insecure, jealous, or anxious.

3. **Post With Purpose**
   – Ask: "Am I expressing or impressing?"

4. **Reply Later, Not Instantly**
   – Don't let your nervous system stay on high alert waiting for replies.

5. **Tech-Free Zone Daily**
   – One hour a day, no screens. Let your other senses breathe.

🖋 Mini Challenge: Online Audit

For one day, note:

- Everything you see online
- How it made you feel
- If it helped or harmed your energy/self-image

You'll be shocked how much passive input is shaping your identity.

🧠 Reframe: Real Over Perfect

Let's shift your mindset:

- From "Likes = Worth" → "Truth = Power"
- From "More followers = More value" → "More **self-knowing** = Real value"

- From “Highlight reel” → “Human reel”

📢 Quotes You Can Share - #teensimage

- “Don’t trade the real you for digital applause.”
- “Be someone worth unfollowing if it means being true to yourself.”
- “You’re not your username. You’re your awareness.”
- “The most powerful post? The one you didn’t need to edit your soul for.”

📶 Progress Gauge.

16.

Friendships & Dating

Emotional Boundaries, Sensory Chemistry & Real Connection

🔗 Introduction: Why Do We "Vibe" With Some People?

Have you ever met someone and instantly felt comfortable?
Or someone else who drained your energy without even doing anything wrong?

That's not just personality. That's **sensory chemistry**.

Your body—and your IMAGE—responds to people through **TEENS**:

Sense	In Friendships/Dating
👀 Eyes	Looks, gestures, body language
👂 Ears	Tone, words, compliments
👃 Nose	Natural scent, emotional memory

Tongue	Conversations, affirmations, teasing
Skin	Hugs, handshakes, touch, space

Without realizing it, your senses are building emotional bonds.

But sometimes, they also build **emotional traps**.

🚦 Connection vs. Confusion

Friendship and dating can be beautiful experiences—or deeply confusing ones.
Here's where most teens go wrong:

- They confuse **attention** with **affection**
- They mistake **touch** for **trust**
- They chase **validation** instead of **values**

Your IMAGE can get hijacked by someone else's energy if you don't know your **emotional boundaries**.

🛡️ Emotional Boundaries: The Invisible Armor

A boundary isn't a wall—it's a **line of self-respect**.

It sounds like:

- "I don't feel comfortable talking about that right now."

- "I need some time to think before I reply."
- "Please don't joke like that about me."

When you **don't have boundaries**, you:

- Overgive and feel drained
- Say yes when you mean no
- Lose your sense of self trying to please others

When you **do have boundaries**, you:

- Attract healthier connections
- Communicate better
- Build relationships that **nourish your IMAGE**, not drain it

---

🔍 Check Yourself: How Are Your Sensory Relationships?

Let's sense-check your relationships using the TEENS lens:

- 👀 Do they look at you with respect? Or judgement?
- 👂 Do their words uplift you? Or make you doubt yourself?
- 👃 Does your time with them leave a good "emotional scent"?

- 👅 Do conversations feel like freedom—or fear of being judged?
- 🫁 Do you feel safe in their presence—or pressured to behave a certain way?

The way someone makes you feel **after they leave** tells you more than what they say while they're around.

💗 Real Chemistry is More Than Looks

Looks may start the connection.
But real chemistry is when:

- You can be silent and still feel seen
- You don't feel drained after talking
- You don't need to perform to be accepted

That's **soul-level resonance**, not just sensory stimulation.

🚨 Red Flags to Watch For (Especially in Dating)

- They constantly check your phone or location
- They comment on how you dress or look—negatively
- They ignore your "no" or make fun of your limits
- They apologize often but **repeat the same behavior**

These aren't signs of "intensity." They're signs of **emotional invasion**.

🌱 What Healthy Friendship/Dating Looks Like

- **Space to grow**
- **Support for your goals**
- **Freedom to express without fear**
- **Respect for your time, choices, and feelings**

The right people don't change your core—they help you discover it.

💬 Powerful Reflection Questions

Ask yourself:

- Do I feel like **more of myself** when I'm with them?
- Can I say **no** without fear?
- Are we **growing together**—or is only one of us doing the work?

💥 The Biggest Myth: "They'll Change"

One of the biggest traps teens fall into is **hope-based connection**.
"If I love them enough, they'll change."
"If I tolerate this, maybe they'll see my worth."

But here's the truth:

> Love doesn't change people. **Self-awareness does.**
> You can support them—but you can't fix them.

The best relationships don't require you to **sacrifice yourself**.

🧠 Rewire Your IMAGE in Relationships

Your relationships should reflect your **inner IMAGE**—your values, awareness, and self-respect.

Set a new standard:

- Don't just look for "vibes"
- Look for **emotional alignment**
- Choose **people who feel like peace**, not pressure

📢 Quotes You Can Share - #teensimage

- "Attraction pulls you in. Awareness keeps you safe."
- "You don't need to be liked by everyone. You need to be respected by yourself."
- "The most beautiful chemistry is calm, not chaos."
- "If you have to shrink to be loved—it's not love. It's control."

📶 Progress Gauge.

17.

Mental Health Awareness

How Sensory Overload Affects Stress—and How to Clean Your Emotional Hygiene

---

🌀 The Overloaded Teen Brain

Let's be real—your mind is not a storage room.
But most teens are using it like one.

Every day, you're hit with:

- Notifications 🛎️
- Loud classrooms 📢
- Overthinking conversations 💬
- Exam pressure 📚
- Music, reels, ads, gossip, noise 🎧

That's called **sensory overload**—when your five senses are absorbing more than your nervous system can handle.
And the result?

You're tired.
You're stressed.
You feel emotionally full—but mentally empty.

What Is Sensory Overload?

Imagine your mind as a cup. Each sound, word, light, touch, smell, and even your own thoughts **pours into it**.
But if you never pour anything out?

Overflow.
That overflow becomes:

- Anxiety
- Overwhelm
- Sudden anger
- Random tears
- Foggy thinking
- "I don't know what's wrong with me" feeling

It's not just "bad mood." It's **clogged senses**.

How TEENS Senses Affect Mental Health

Sense	Stress Trigger
Tongue	Harsh self-talk, constant talking, junk food

Eyes	Scrolling, screen time, comparing yourself
Ears	Loud environments, negative people, criticism
Nose	Smells that remind you of past traumas or environments
Skin	Lack of rest, overstimulation, physical discomfort

Your **IMAGE** is not just shaped by what you consume.
It's also shaped by **what you don't detox.**

What Is Emotional Hygiene?

You brush your teeth.
You bathe your body.
But when was the last time you **cleaned your emotions**?

Emotional hygiene =
→ Noticing when you're overloaded
→ Taking time to unplug and reset
→ Letting your senses relax

Small Inputs, Big Effects

Your nervous system is like a sponge. Even small things build up:

- One toxic comment from a friend
- One negative news headline

- One hour too long on a screen
- One moment of holding back tears

Over time, these **micro-inputs** become **macro-mental problems**.

✋ Signs You Need a Break

- Everything feels loud—even silence
- You feel easily irritated
- You're scrolling without feeling anything
- You want to be alone—but also don't
- You can't hear your own thoughts anymore

This isn't laziness.
It's your **nervous system asking for help**.

🔧 Reboot Your Inner System: Emotional Reset Routine

1. **Silence Mode (10 minutes)**
   No music, no talking, no phone.
   Just sit. Let your system breathe.

2. **Breathe Deeply (3 minutes)**
   Inhale for 4, hold for 4, exhale for 6.
   This calms the amygdala—your brain's panic button.

3. **Journaling Dump (5 minutes)**
   Write everything that's in your head.
   Even if it's messy, even if it's stupid.
   Get it out of your brain and onto paper.

4. **Grounding Senses (2 minutes)**
   Notice:

   - 5 things you can see 👀
   - 4 things you can touch 👐
   - 3 things you can hear 👂
   - 2 things you can smell 👃
   - 1 thing you can taste 👅

This resets your nervous system and brings your awareness back into your body.

🧘 Emotional Rest ≠ Sleeping

Sometimes you sleep and still feel tired.
That's because your **mind hasn't rested.**

What it needs isn't just sleep.
It needs **disconnection from noise** and **reconnection with self**.

📱 Screen Detox Is Mental Detox

Your screen is the loudest voice in your life.
If you never unplug, you're never fully present.

Try this:

- 1 hour a day: **screen-free block**
- 1 day a week: **slow-down Sunday**
- 1 week a year: **digital minimalism reset**

You'll feel lighter—not because life changed—but because your **senses finally got space**.

🌱 Be Gentle With Yourself

Mental health isn't about being happy all the time.
It's about:

- Being **aware** of what's going on inside
- Having tools to **rebalance**
- Giving yourself **permission to pause**

You don't need to "fix" everything overnight.
You just need to start **listening to your inner signals**.

💬 Reflection Prompts

- What sensory input is overwhelming me right now?
- When was the last time I gave myself quiet time?
- What activities **drain** me, and what activities **refill** me?

📢 Quotes You Can Share - #teensimage

- "Just because your phone recharges daily doesn't mean you do."
- "Emotional hygiene is self-love in practice."
- "Silence is not empty. It's full of answers."
- "Mental clarity begins where sensory overload ends."

📊 Progress Gauge.

18.

Confidence & Public IMAGE

Posture, Tone, Clothes, Energy—How to Carry Your IMAGE Confidently

---

🎭 What People See Is Not Always What You Feel

Let's be honest.
You could feel super nervous inside—
—but if you stand tall, speak clearly, and walk with intention, people will still see confidence.

Why?

Because confidence isn't just a feeling.
It's a **sensory signal**.

Your TEENS senses send cues to the world—and to your own brain—about how confident you are.

🔍 How TEENS Affects Confidence

Sense	How It Builds (or Breaks) Confidence

👀 Eyes	Eye contact = presence; comparison = self-doubt
👂 Ears	How you talk to yourself; tone of voice
👃 Nose	Scents connected to calm or anxiety
👅 Tongue	Words you use—positive, honest, respectful
👐 Skin	Posture, body language, movement

ConfidenceConfidence isn't just a **personality trait**—
It's a **practice**.
A language.
A physical habit.

👤 Inner IMAGE vs. Public IMAGE

- **Inner IMAGE** = What you believe about yourself
- **Public IMAGE** = What others perceive about you

Here's the secret:

> The more aligned these two are, the more powerful your confidence becomes.

Fake confidence is exhausting.
Real confidence feels like **freedom**.

💬 Your Voice = Your Vibe

Tone is a **vibe amplifier**.
You might be saying "I'm fine,"
but your tone says "I'm nervous, please like me."

Train your tone:

- Practice reading aloud with calm, steady rhythm
- Avoid ending sentences like a question unless it is one
- Drop your shoulders—your voice flows better from a relaxed body

---

🧍 Posture is Psychology

The way you stand **changes your state of mind.**

Try this:

- Slouch down, fold your arms, look down.
  You feel small, right?

Now:

- Stand tall, roll shoulders back, breathe deep.
  You feel like you have space.

This isn't imagination. It's **embodied confidence**.

👕 Style as a Statement

Your clothes are your **visual language**.

Wearing what makes you feel:

- Clear
- Aligned
- Comfortable
- True to your vibe

...transmits authenticity.

It's not about brands.
It's about **intention behind appearance**.

Ask:

> "Am I dressing to express or to impress?"

💡 Energy Speaks Before You Do

Before you say a word, people feel your energy.

Confident energy isn't:

- Loud
- Arrogant
- Over-dominant

Confident energy is:

- Calm

- Grounded
- Present
- Aware of others, not just self

You don't need to control the room.
Just **own your space**.

🧠 Reprogramming Confidence Through Senses

Want to grow real confidence? Use TEENS consciously:

- 👀 Mirror check with affirmations: "I belong here."
- 👂 Record your voice. Learn to love its sound.
- 👃 Use calming scents before high-stress events.
- 👅 Practice clear, honest self-talk. Speak what you stand for.
- 👐 Take up space. Walk like you've already arrived.

🔁 The Confidence Loop

Confidence → Better posture, tone, and energy → Positive reactions from people → Reinforced self-image → More confidence

But it also works in reverse.
Negative posture → Negative reaction → Lower confidence

Break that loop by becoming **sensorily aware**.

🧩 Final IMAGE Tip: Don't Perform. Align.

People can feel when you're trying too hard.

You don't have to be perfect.
You just have to be:

- **Present**
- **Purposeful**
- **Peaceful in your own skin**

That's real power.

🧭 Confidence Isn't Just About You

True confidence uplifts others.
It walks in a room and says:

> "You're safe here."
> "You're seen."
> "We're equal."

That's the IMAGE that transforms spaces.

📢 Quotes You Can Share - #teensimage

- "Confidence isn't volume. It's vibration."
- "You don't need to shrink to fit in. You need to expand to stand out."
- "Posture is the silent voice of your mindset."
- "People won't always remember what you said—but they'll never forget how your energy felt."

📶 Progress Gauge.

📕 PART 4 SUMMARY

"This is where your IMAGE steps into real life."

You've built self-awareness. You've reshaped your habits and mindset.
Now it's time to apply your IMAGE in five important areas of daily teen life—
school, screens, friendships, emotions, and public confidence.

📖 Chapter 14: TEENS IMAGE at School

"School tests more than your memory—it tests your self-image."

- School is a **sensory battlefield**—with noise, pressure, comparisons, and emotion.
- It's not your marks, but your **reaction** to those marks that shape your IMAGE.
- Two students. Same failure. Different mindset = Different future.

🛠 **Activity:** Compare your "School Self" vs "Home Self"
💬 *Quote: "Your rank is temporary. Your reaction becomes your reality."*

📱 Chapter 15: Social Media & Digital Persona

"The real you is not a filter."

- What you see online becomes a **downloaded belief** into your inner image.
- Social media triggers dopamine through likes—but also insecurity through comparison.
- You don't need to quit. You need to **design your digital space with awareness**.

🛠 **Tools:** Online Audit, Digital Boundaries
💬 Quote: "Don't trade the real you for digital applause."

🖤 Chapter 16: Friendships & Dating

- You connect through your **TEENS senses**: words, looks, touch, scent, energy.
- Real bonds respect boundaries. Fake ones drain your IMAGE.
- If someone makes you shrink to feel loved—it's not love, it's control.
- Connections should feel calm, not confusion."

🛠 **Tool:** Sensory Relationship Check + Red Flag Awareness
💬 *Quote: "Attraction pulls you in. Awareness keeps you safe."*

🧠 Chapter 17: Mental Health Awareness

"Your brain isn't broken—it's just overloaded."

- Constant input (sounds, screens, noise, pressure) leads to **sensory overload**.
- Your mind needs breaks, just like your body.
- **Emotional hygiene** means noticing, pausing, and resetting.

🛠 **Tool:** Emotional Reset Routine (Silence, Breath, Dump, Grounding)
💬 *Quote: "Mental clarity begins where sensory overload ends."*

✨ Chapter 18: Confidence & Public IMAGE

- Confidence is a **sensory language**: posture, tone, presence.
- When your **inner image** and **public image** match, you feel peace—not pressure.
- You don't need to perform. You need to **own your space with calm energy**.
- *"Confidence isn't loud. It's aligned."*

🛠 **Tool:** Confidence Loop + Reprogram with TEENS
💬 *Quote: "Posture is the silent voice of your mindset."*

Final Message of Part 4:

You're not just thinking differently now—you're living differently.
The world won't always change for you.
But now, with the right IMAGE, **you show up differently to the world.**

19.

Create Your IMAGE Vision Board

Your Future—Seen Before It Happens

Imagine this…

You walk into your room and see a board filled with images:

- A smiling, confident version of you
- A calm morning routine
- A clean plate of colorful food
- A powerful quote like:

> "I shape my life by shaping my senses."

You pause. You breathe.
And your brain whispers—**"That's who I'm becoming."**

That's the power of a **Vision Board**.

🧠 Why Visuals Work on Your Mind

Your brain is wired to respond to **images**.
Words may explain. But **images make you feel**.
They activate your **emotion**, **memory**, and **action centers**—
Without overthinking.

When you see a picture of your future every day,
Your brain starts searching for ways to **make it real.**
That's why we're creating this board—not just for inspiration…
But for transformation.

📋 What Is an IMAGE Vision Board?

This isn't some magical poster.
It's your **personal dashboard**.

> A snapshot of your **Inner & Outer IMAGE**
> Made up of visuals, words, reminders, and small habits.

It's a **mirror** of the person you're building,
And a **map** to remind you how to get there.

🧩 Step-by-Step: Build Your IMAGE Vision Board

1. Start with 2 Questions:

- "Who do I want to become?"
- "What habits, inputs, and environments will shape that?"

Write the answers roughly in a notebook first.
This is the **raw data** of your future self.

2. Divide Your Board into 6 Zones: (TEENS + IMAGE)

Zone	Focus
T: Tongue	What do I want to eat more mindfully? What words should I say to myself and others?
E: Eyes	What visuals do I want more of? What should I stop watching?
E: Ears	What kind of music, voices, and sounds lift me up?
N: Nose	What scents make me feel alive or safe?
S: Skin	What kind of environments feel comforting, energizing, or clean?
IMAGE (Inner + Outer)	What is my dream self-image? What clothes, posture, attitude reflect that?

3. Gather Visuals

- **Magazines, Pinterest, Canva, Newspapers, Doodles**
- Pick:
    - **Photos of role models**
    - **Power words**: Discipline, Calm, Courage
    - **Habits in pictures**: yoga, journaling, drinking water
    - **Your own photo**, smiling and strong
- Add symbols or art that speak to you—this is your vibe.

4. Don’t Just Dream—Break It Into Action

Under each image, add a small **habit or ritual**.

Example:

> 🧘 Image: A peaceful morning scene
> ✅ Action: “10-minute silence before school”
>
> 🥗 Image: A clean plate of vegetables
> ✅ Action: “Drink water first before any craving”

These micro-habits build your **macro-vision**.

---

5. Place It Where You’ll See It Every Day

Stick it:

- On your wall
- Inside your wardrobe
- As your phone wallpaper (digital version)

Why?
Because **daily exposure = deeper belief**.
Repetition makes the dream familiar. Familiar becomes achievable.

🧠 **Science Check:**

Did you know your **Reticular Activating System (RAS)** filters what your brain notices?

If you tell your brain daily:

"I am becoming strong, focused, joyful,"
It starts filtering your world through that lens.

A Vision Board **programs your RAS** to spot:

- Better choices
- Right people
- Powerful habits

You'll start seeing **your IMAGE** unfold.

✨ **Your Board. Your Story. Your Future.**

This is not about being perfect.
It's about being **intentional.**
It's not just about seeing your dream life—
It's about becoming the kind of person who can live it.

A Fun Twist:

Take a photo of your board.
Share it.
Make it your lock screen.
Stick it on your mirror.
Let the world slowly catch up with who you're becoming.

> **"I don't wait for the future. I create it—with one vision and one habit at a time."**

Challenge 🔥

"Build your IMAGE Board and look at it daily for 30 days."
Track:
✅ What changed in your decisions?
✅ What habits became easier?
✅ How did you feel about yourself?

Ready to build?

Take your scissors, phone, pen, and your dreams—
Let's shape what the world will soon see.

📢 Quotes You Can Share - #teensimage

- "I don't wait for the future. I create it—with one vision and one habit at a time."
- "Your future is already whispering—are you listening?"
- "A clear vision pulls you forward when motivation fades."
- "What you see every day, you start to believe. What you believe, you begin to become."
- "If you don't shape your vision, the world will shape it for you."

📶 Progress Gauge.

95%

20.

Walking Together – Final Words

"If you've seen my IMAGE, I'm walking with you."

Dear Reader,

By now, you've explored your senses...
You've paused to reflect...
You've decoded your habits...
You've begun shaping your inner and outer IMAGE...

And through it all, you weren't alone.

> You were walking with me—and more importantly,
> **you were walking with yourself.**

This Isn't the End. It's the Real Beginning.

This book may end here,
But your IMAGE is alive—
It grows every day, with every choice, every input, every step.

There's no "final version" of you.
There's just one question you'll keep asking:

> "What kind of person am I becoming?"

If You've Seen My IMAGE...

You've seen a teenager who once struggled with decisions.
You've seen someone confused by cravings, distracted by noise, shaped by screens...
But who woke up.
Who studied the senses, the habits, the inputs...
Who experimented, failed, journaled, paused, and reprogrammed.

You've seen **my IMAGE evolve**.

And now—

> If you've seen it clearly,
> **You're already walking with me.**

A Book You Can Revisit, Not Just Read Once

This is not a book to finish and forget.
It's a book to return to—when life gets loud, when the world pulls you away from yourself.

Some chapters will mean more later.
Some parts may hit deeper a year from now.
That's perfect.

Your IMAGE will keep unfolding.
So keep checking in. Keep shaping it.

One Final Gift: The TEENS IMAGE Life Lens

Before you go, here's a simple mantra you can whisper daily:

> **"What I see, hear, say, smell, taste, and feel—becomes my IMAGE."**
> **"So I choose what enters. I choose what I become."**

That's all you need.

To the One Walking Ahead

You're not just a teen.
You're a **creator**—of your energy, your expression, your evolution.

Keep walking.
Keep observing.
Keep becoming.

Because the world isn't waiting for someone perfect.
It's waiting for someone **conscious**.

> Someone like you.

With You, Always

—Vishal Tiwari
Author of TEENS IMAGE

> "I shaped my **IMAGE**.
> Now it's your turn **Baccha**."

📢 Quotes You Can Share - #teensimage

- "You don't finish shaping your IMAGE. You grow with it—every choice, every day."

- "This isn't the end of a book. It's the beginning of your conscious life."

- "The world doesn't need perfection. It needs presence. It needs people like you—awake and evolving."

- "If you've seen my IMAGE, you're not just reading my story—you're remembering your own."

- "You're not just a teen. You're the architect of your attention, your actions, your becoming."

📶 Progress Gauge.

100%

🌟 FINAL PART SUMMARY

> *"You've sensed it, shaped it, now it's time to see it—and live it."*

This part turns your self-awareness into a **daily visual anchor** and gives you a **clear message for the road ahead**.
You've gone from **passive input → conscious choice → personal transformation**. Now you **design your future**.

📖 Chapter 19: Create Your IMAGE Vision Board

> *"Don't just dream your IMAGE—see it, speak it, and step into it."*

- Your brain understands visuals better than words—use that to your advantage.
- A Vision Board programs your **Reticular Activating System (RAS)** to focus on goals, not distractions.
- Build your board using the **TEENS senses** and **Inner/Outer IMAGE** zones.
- *"Don't just dream your IMAGE—see it, speak it, and step into it."*

🧩 **6 Zones to Map**:

Zone	What You Design
👅 Tongue	Food, affirmations, self-talk

👁 Eyes	Visuals to see, media to avoid
👂 Ears	Uplifting sounds, music, silence
👃 Nose	Comfort scents, triggers to heal
✋ Skin	Safe environments, physical rest
💫 IMAGE	Posture, clothing, energy, mindset

🛠 **Add under each image:**

- Small actions (e.g. "10 mins silence," "affirmation before mirror")

📌 **Daily Use = Deep Programming**
Looking at it each day rewires what your brain sees as "normal" and possible.

💬 *Quote: "Repetition makes the dream familiar. Familiar becomes achievable."*
🔥 *Challenge:* Use it for 30 days and track what changes.

👣 Chapter 20: Walking Together – Final Words

"This isn't the end. It's the beginning of becoming."

- Your IMAGE is not a destination—it's a direction.

- You've explored your senses, shaped your habits, and reflected on your identity.
- Now it's time to **walk forward with presence and power**.

🧠 **The Daily Mantra**:

> *"What I see, hear, say, smell, taste, and feel—becomes my IMAGE.*
> *So I choose what enters. I choose what I become."*

💬 *Quote: "You're not just a teen. You're a creator—of your energy, your evolution."*

This closing reminds the reader:
They are not alone. They are not behind. They are **already becoming**.

🔑 FINAL MESSAGE

> **You shaped your IMAGE—and now, your IMAGE shapes your life.**
> Your board is your mirror.
> Your senses are your toolkit.
> Your choices are your future.

About the Author

Vishal Tiwari – Author of TEENS IMAGE Hi, my name is **Vishal Tiwari** 🙋‍♂️, and I'm a 24-year-old seeker, entrepreneur, and now, author. My journey began not with books 📚, but with blessings—from my grandfather, the Late **Umrao Tiwari** 👴, and my father, **Mr. Vivek Kumar Tiwari** 👨‍👦. From childhood, I was introduced to timeless spiritual concepts like **Man** (🧠 Perceiving Mind), **Buddhi** (🧩 Intellect), **Vivek** (⚖️ Discernment), and **Chetna** (💡 Conscious Awareness). These weren't just words for me—they were tools I would later use to decode the chaos of life 🌪️.

After completing my education 🎓, I stepped into the real world—the battlefield of dreams and demands ⚔️. It was there I had a realization: *What if the information we constantly receive through our five senses—the* ***TEENS*** *(👅 Tongue, 👀 Eyes, 👂 Ears, 👃 Nose, ✋ Skin)—is not random, but actually shaping us?* What if we could control it—and in doing so, reshape ourselves? 🔄

I decided to experiment 🧪. I tried these ideas in different areas of life—health, habits, relationships, learning—and saw real transformation 🌱. Then came the final test: business 💼. I poured in my focus, filtered my sensory inputs toward entrepreneurial growth 📈, and saw success 🌟. One day, during a conversation with a client 🤝, he said, *"Can you be my Executive Assistant?"* I replied, *"I'm already running my business."* He smiled and said, *"Do both. I'll help you in your field, and you help me in mine."*

That moment taught me something powerful:

> 💬 **Every success has its own field—and every field has its own parameters. When you fulfill those parameters, the field becomes yours.** ✅

And how do you fulfill those parameters? By filtering, focusing, and mastering the information you absorb through your TEENS 👁️‍🗨️. Once you do that, your *IMAGE*—the person you become—naturally aligns with the life you desire 🎯.

This book isn't about a fancy theory or a new trend 🚫. Everything in it is already known to you—because it's natural 🌿. I've just given it a name and a path: **TEENS IMAGE** 🌄.

Let's walk this path together 👣.